FINAL WARNING

By

George Jenkins

ISBN: 978-0-9939070-7-4

All Scripture references taken from the King James Version unless otherwise stated!

Italics mine – used only to accent!

"Blow ye the trumpet in Zion, and sound an alarm in my holy mountain: let all the inhabitants of the land tremble: for the day of the LORD cometh, for it is nigh at hand." (Joel 2:1)

Table of Contents

DEDICATION

This book I dedicate to all those who have positively impacted my life. Those, who in love challenged me to dig deeper into the heart of the Word of God. Those who taught me never to settle for less than God's very best.

Some of those wonderful people have given many hours, days, working tirelessly, reading and editing this manuscript. Without them this book would not have been possible.

Above all else, I give the production of this book to Jesus. All the truths contained in this work are His and only His to direct into the hands of those He wants to read them.

Some have asked me what the Lord will give me next to write. My answer is simple! The time is so short, there may not be time to write another.

In conclusion, I dedicate this book to you, those who will read it and who will run with haste to Jesus, before it's too late.

FOREWORD

"Final Warning" is a critical exposé, on the deceptions of Satan, for the true blood bought, blood washed, children of God, the end time's church and the whole world.

It carries the reader through a wide range of subjects building to a crescendo of excitement with every page turned. Skillfully, George Jenkins carries us through world events and right into our last days on earth. Along the way he blows the whistle on false doctrine, false manifestations of the presence of Christ, false forms of ministry practiced, false apostles, prophets and teachers in the church today. He opens up to the reader the truth on many of the so-called manifestations flying around in renewal circles.

In this work, Satan is totally exposed for who and what he is, the master of deception. So cunning are his ways that even the elect are in danger!

It confronts the failure of the Bible prophet, Balaam, and brings out the serious warnings of Scripture against "The way of Balaam," a readiness to prostitute his higher spiritual gifts and privileges for personal gain. "The error of Balaam," a willingness to compromise his own morality and truth for popularity and "The doctrine of Balaam," the use of position and influence to persuade others that they can compromise standards and truth for false manifestations of Jesus. This is nothing less than spiritual adultery that exists today.

The signs of the heavens are clearly presented!

When you have seen the manifest glory of God, come down in a service, where ministry ceased and a victory dance exploded, you will know why cheap misrepresentations like golden glitter, orbs of light, angel feathers can never replace His presence.

"Final Warning" is a compassionate cry from the broken heart of a man of God, a true prophet, willing to confront, to expose, and to risk popularity for the truth, for God's glory!

The cry is to wake up! Wake up believers! Wake up church! Be alert! Be on guard! Satan as a roaring lion goes about seeking to devour all he can.

George shows us what to do if we discover our church caught in deception. Recognize these deceptions for what they are compared to the whole counsel of the Word of God! Reject these deceptions out of hand! Repent where needed and return to the true gospel, the true Jesus, to true worship and to the true program of God in these final hours!

"Final Warning," I could not put the book down. Page after page is filled with a mysterious excitement leading to the exposure of the beast and false prophet of Revelation. Turning the last page of the book, I was compelled to look up, convinced that the end is here! The trumpet is about to sound! This is a must-read book for every believer! It's vivid, poignant, and absorbing!

Rev. Ralph Dunn B.Th.
Senior Pastor
The Bridegroom's House
Kitchener, Ont. Canada

INTRODUCTION

A quick glance around the globe should convince us that the time of the end is at hand. In fact, it stands at the very door. Should this concern us! Definitely YES! In more ways than one! Today the Lord is sending out one, "Final Warning," that the end is upon us! How can we know this?

"The coming of the lawless one will be accompanied by the power of Satan. He will use every kind of power, including miraculous signs, lying wonders." (2 Thessalonians 2:9)

Then, Jesus said:

"For there shall arise false Christs, and false prophets, and shall shew great signs and wonders; insomuch that, if it were possible, they shall deceive the very elect." (Matthew 24:24)

Is the beast and false prophet of Revelation already in our midst? YES! Are their counterfeits all around us today? YES! Are they in our churches? YES! Where can they be found? How can we protect ourselves from the lies of the enemy?

"You will know the truth, and the truth will make you free." (John 8:32)

How can we know if the manifestations we are experiencing in our church meetings are God's best? How can we know if what we hear from our pulpits is from the heart of God?

"Now the Bereans were more noble-minded than the Thessalonians, for they received the message with great eagerness and examined the Scriptures every day to see if these teachings were true." (Acts 17:11)

"Final Warning," offers insight, into all that is going on in our day! Where we are going in this book and its conclusion, will help us understand how the enemy works and how Jesus will overcome him in the end.

As we search for truth, we will discover that many false doctrines have taken to the church stage. Doctrines that have come down throughout the years and remain in many churches even today. Errors that form a pattern and part of a greater plan, designed by hell for our day.

The enemy works by infiltrating the church here a little and there a little, over the years. With each step he carries believers, one step at a time, further and further away from, "the whole counsel of God." Then too, some of his lies he designs for detection, so that other aspects of his plan go undetected. The more he infiltrates the church, the easier it becomes for believers to buy into another error. When discovered, it sometimes takes generations to remove the embedded wrong. Since fragments remain, they open the door for the later introduction of more error. Evils that are particularly tuned for our day to reach, and confuse people, at the point of their need.

What can we do? What should we do, if we discover our church, caught by deception?

"Come out from among them, and be ye separate and touch not the unclean thing." (2 Corinthians 6:17)

That's much easier said than done! It's heartbreaking to know that the expositors of error have deceived many. People have invested years, coming to accept what they believe as truth. At Prayer Meetings, Bible Studies, House Groups, Women's Ministries, Men's Breakfasts and Church services, they dedicated their time to attend. Without knowing, they are innocent victims drowning in a sea of doctrinal oversight.

As with many drowning people, they thrash and fight their rescuer! Just imagine that all our life they told us something was right, only to have someone else come along and tell us that it does not line up with Scripture. Naturally, there will be a reaction. We feel deceived by our pastors and church leaders. Some may not realize that they too were taken in by others. We may even wonder how we can ever become vulnerable again after such a betrayal. It is for all these, I am deeply concerned for, as I begin to write.

"Final Warning," is more than a survival guide for the end times. It's designed to help you seek for and to move into the great and mighty things you know nothing about. (Jeremiah 33:3)

Its purpose is to open our eyes to all that is going on around us, to see how close to the end we really are.

Then, the LORD said, "Shall I hide from Abraham what I am about to do?" (Genesis 18:17)

Since we are the seed of Abraham, the same applies to us! The Lord wants you to know clearly all that He is doing in our time!

The last great finale of the church on earth has begun!

FINDING THE TEN TRIBES

All around the globe, many are asking where the lost ten tribes of Israel's northern kingdom are. The prophecies of the regathering show us that these tribes will play a major part in the fulfillment of many other prophecies. Revelations about world events before Jesus returns to set up the Kingdom of God on earth. Others wonder since Israel was scattered, did God cast them off? Even more preposterously, some say that the LORD has abandoned Israel and replaced her with the church! Nonsense!

His covenant with Israel is sure and certain. He reiterated it through Moses, repeated it by the prophets and rehearsed it by the psalmists. Jesus Himself affirmed it (Matthew 19:28), Paul articulated it (Romans 9-11) and the gates of the New Jerusalem announce it forever. (Revelation 21:11-12) God has chosen Israel as His covenant people.

What if Israel broke the covenant? What would happen to them then? Listen to these unmistakably clear truths:

"Though I completely destroy all the nations among which I scatter you, I will not completely destroy you. I will discipline you but only with justice; I will not let you go entirely unpunished." (Jeremiah 30:11b *paraphrased*)

God will completely destroy other nations, but He will not completely destroy Israel! He treats His people differently from other people; He judges them more strictly, but they will never be wiped out.

No matter what Israel does, God will never forsake them as His distinct people. In Jeremiah 31:31-34, the Lord declares that He will make a new covenant with Israel and Judah. Then, He doesn't stop there. It's as if He's saying, 'Now, don't get me wrong! Don't think that this new covenant means that I'm abandoning my people. NO!'

"Thus saith the LORD, which giveth the sun for a light by day, and the ordinances of the moon and of the stars for a light by night, which divideth the sea when the waves thereof roar; The LORD of hosts is his name:

If those ordinances depart from before me, saith the LORD, then the seed of Israel also shall cease from being a nation before me forever.

Thus saith the LORD; if heaven above can be measured, and the foundations of the earth searched out beneath, I will also cast off all the seed of Israel for all that they have done, saith the LORD." (Jeremiah. 31:35-37)

If you are still uncertain about the calling of Israel, consider this simple truth: If God could forsake Israel, in spite of His unconditional, everlasting promises, then He could forsake the Church! If God could replace Israel, in spite of His absolute, eternal promises, then He could replace the Church! So, if we hold to a theology that says, "God has forsaken physical Israel," or "The Church has replaced Israel," we had better be extremely careful!

So where are the lost ten tribes of Israel? Let's begin with a promise the LORD gave to the House of Israel.

"Therefore prophesy and say unto them, Thus saith the Lord GOD; Behold, O my people, I will open your graves, and cause you to come up out of your graves, and bring you into the land of Israel." (Ezekiel 37:12)

All through Scripture, the prophets declared that God would bring back, "the apple of His eye," to the Promised Land. (Jeremiah 33, Zachariah 2:8) This is evolving right before our eyes. According to Eliezer Ben-Yehuda, "1881" was a significant year in the history of Israel. In that year the Hebrew language was restored to the people. This was the fulfilment of the prophecy of Zephaniah 3:9a.

"For then will I turn to the people a pure language that they may all call upon the name of the LORD."

As the people began to return, Theodor Herzl, the father of Zionism who was the first to bring about restoration to Israel in 1948, set about a system of retaining. The prophecies of Israel returning to the Promised Land did not come about overnight. After their return, they had to learn many things dealing with what belonged to them as citizens of the State of Israel. Jeremiah spoke of these days of glory.

"Behold, I will send for many fishers, saith the LORD, and they shall fish them; and after will I send for many hunters, and they shall hunt them from every mountain, and from every hill, and out of the holes of the rocks." (Jeremiah 16:16)

This Scripture, in speaking of Israel, describes the rebirth of the nation. It speaks of men like Theodor Herzl, who sent out people searching the nations to discover and return the dispersed Jews to their Promised Land.

Travelling the world the fishermen landed in just about every nation on the face of the earth. From Iran 30,000 Jews returned home. From Russia one million. Latin America 10,000, France 13,000, and North America 200,000. The last group of Ethiopian Jews, some 450 so-called "Falashas" flew to an airport near Tel Aviv in two chartered flights, sixty-five years after the birth of the Israeli nation. The country has now concluded its mass repatriation program for Ethiopian Jews. From country after country the world over, Jews went home. Even from Ireland 785 returned to Israel!

In 2013, the office of the Prime Minister of Israel announced that some people "wishing to immigrate to Israel could be subjected to DNA testing to prove their Jewishness." A Foreign Ministry official said that the genetic testing program was based on the recommendations of an Israeli government organization that has helped Jews from Russia and the rest of the former Soviet Union with immigration since the 1950s.

What about the rest? Among the great mysteries studied by historians and theologians for centuries has been the fate of the so-called "Lost Tribes of Israel." We know the outcome of the Jews taken from the Kingdom of Judah (*the southern kingdom*) to Babylon. Most of the Jewish people living in Israel today are descendants of those taken to Babylon under King Nebuchadnezzar. They then returned during the reign of Cyrus. This, they confirmed through genetic testing!

However, the Assyrians carried the ten tribes that comprised Israel's Northern Kingdom into captivity more than one hundred years earlier. There they seem to have vanished from memory into the mists of time. (2 Kings 15:29, 2 Kings 17:3-6) Some perhaps intermarried, others may have abandoned their faith, and even more, time just forgot. Time may have forgotten them, but not the LORD!

"And I will gather the remnant of my flock out of all countries whither I have driven them, and will bring them again to their folds; and they shall be fruitful and increase." (Jeremiah 23:3)

Who are they? Reuben, Simeon, Dan, Naphtali, Gad, Asher, Issachar, Zebulun, Ephraim, and Manasseh make up what is now referred to as "The Lost Tribes of Israel." Actually they are far from being lost. The LORD knows exactly where they are!

The Lord continues to launch out His fishermen in search of His children. These Evangelists, in our day are entrusted with travelling to the nations to work for the conversion of the Jews. The work of reaching the chosen people has been hindered by our being distracted by meetings filled with so-called manifestations. Thus, many have missed the call of the hour and only a pitiful few care for Israel. Many say they bless Israel, but few rarely do! Still and for all of this, the LORD says:

"And it shall come to pass in that day, that the Lord shall set his hand again the second time to recover the remnant of his people, which shall be left, from Assyria, and from Egypt, and from Pathros, and from Cush, and from Elam, and from Shinar, and from Hamath, and from the islands of the sea." (Isaiah 11:11)

The search for them began in Africa, and in particular, Ethiopia. In India, among an indigenous group of people, some were found. They had long forgotten their Jewish roots. Then, one night, some of their leaders began having dreams and revelations about who they were as a people. Initially, they returned to the worship of the one true God, and although they had no copies of the Bible to read, many members of this tribe, particularly those living in the state of Mizoram, became Christians. They lived as Christians until the dreams revealed that they were in fact Jewish.

13

Miracle after miracle has brought to light the location of Jews, still returning home. It will be through the supernatural that the needle in the haystack will be found. Without the Holy Spirit it would be impossible. One would think that the church should get excited to jump in on what the LORD is doing in our day. They are not! In fact, many official positions taken by the churches about Israel and Palestine will shock you! Of course, some things can be expected.

In recent months, the Pope convened a Prayer Peace Summit with Israel and the Palestinian Authority. In attendance at that meeting were Syria and the Patriarch of Constantinople, Turkey. Where did that take place? The Vatican, of course! Immediately following this summit, the Pope stabbed Israel in the back! It was prophetic of the betrayal that the Antichrist will bring halfway through the tribulation.

The Pope recognized Palestine as a state. This announcement was a direct attempt to disenfranchise the Jewish people. Meeting with Palestinian officials at the Vatican, church officials agreed to formally recognize the "State of Palestine" as part of a deal concerning Catholic activities in the Palestinian-controlled areas. This outrageous step was a severe blow to Catholic-Jewish relations and it cannot go unanswered by Israel. Nor can it go unanswered by the Bible believing church! Nor will it go unanswered by the LORD!

In biblical terms, by recognizing a Palestinian State in Judea and Samaria, the Vatican is effectively seeking to deny the eternal covenant between God and the Jewish people, to whom this land was given long ago. At the same time, the Pope's counterpart, the Coptic Pope said this about Israel:

14

"Do not believe their claims that they are God's chosen people because it is not true." - Wikipedia

In the light of end time Scripture, we can understand why they did this. What is a tougher pill to swallow is the position taken by other churches. Positions that should shake us, right down to our boots.

The Salvation Army's Captain Rick Zelinsky is the Director of Field Education at the College for Officer Training. Intermingled in his long wandering exegesis of the Israeli-Palestinian debate, he claims in "The Voice of the Salvationist," their official magazine:

"Many Christian Zionist's fail to acknowledge the Palestinian desire, for a legitimate voice and a homeland. This only furthers the conflict that exists in the Middle East. The worst part is that the Christian Zionist movement justifies their support of Israel's cause based on Scripture. How do we speak of God's justice and mercy, grace and hope to a people, (*The Palestinians*) who have experienced hatred, discrimination and injustice in the name of the same God?"

Obviously, in conclusion, the Salvation Army has taken a stand against the return and resettlement of the Jews. Even more horrifying is the fact that his office is one that governs the training of the next generation to fill the pulpit.

What he is forgetting in his challenge to the building of settlements is simple. The land was originally stolen from the Israeli people. It was then passed from one generation to another. The passage of time does not alter the fact that they had committed a crime, it remains stolen property. The Salvation Army is fully aware of this, from their active role in the Criminal Justice Ministry.

15

Many years after the end of World War II, the Jewish people began to reclaim their artwork stolen by the Nazis. Courts all around the world upheld their claims and the items were returned. By then, those who had stolen the artwork in the first place were dead and gone. Their children and their children's children possessed the stolen property and they were eventually returned to the descendants of the rightful property owners.

Another example of the Jew's right to their land, given to them by God, is found in Canada. When the Europeans came to Canada, we disenfranchised the first nation's people of their land. We pushed them further and further into the bush until many lived in swamps. Over the past three decades the courts upheld their claims and had to grant them compensation in the billions. Some lands were returned to the people that God gave them to in the first place. None of this is ever mentioned by the opponents of the settlements in Israel. Most of those antagonists are found within and not outside the church!

The Church of Scotland: In a new report titled "The Inheritance of Abraham? The 'Promised Land,'" the Church of Scotland, once a staunch supporter of the Jew's right to their ancient homeland, says: "Israel does not belong to the Jewish people." Scotland is a land that has known historic revival under the leadership of John Knox. He, so overcome by the state of his nation, cried in prayer. "Give me Scotland or let me die." Obviously we need someone today to take a similar stand.

The Episcopal Church: This church has approximately 2 million members and 7,200 churches in the U.S. alone and is part of the 77-million member

16

Anglican Communion. Miserably, the Episcopal Church is not a trustworthy observer of the Arab-Israeli conflict. The church's leaders and constitutive bodies routinely issue one-sided statements about the Arab-Israeli conflict, and its publications portray Israel as exclusively responsible for violence in the region.

The Lutheran Church, founded by the great Martin Luther: Evangelical Lutheran Church in America (*ELCA*). The ELCA is very anti-Israel. They actively promote a boycott against Israeli made goods and against companies that sell to them. They use coded language and try to make themselves sound like they seek peace for Palestine and Israel, but they have a view of peace that only goes along with the Palestinian demands.

John and Charles Wesley's Methodists: In late June 2010, the Methodist Church in Britain, the fourth largest Christian denomination in the UK with 70 million members worldwide, voted to boycott Israeli-produced goods and services from the West Bank because of what they call, Israel's "illegal occupation of Palestinian lands."

The United Methodists were among the first to attack Israel economically by selling off their financial holdings in Israel. They published a statement:

"Does Israel Practice Apartheid?" "The very definition of apartheid is controversial. In its simplest terms, it means separation, or more precisely a separation of peoples. There is no doubt that Israel has operated on this principle in the occupied territories. Due to Israel's settlement policy, two peoples are spread throughout the Holy Land. One group has rights and privileges, plentiful water and segregated roadways. The other group has few rights, inadequate water and no ability to stop the first group from confiscating its land." - United Methodists' Holy Land Task Force is a member organization of the US Campaign to End the Israeli Occupation.

The Presbyterians: In 2004, the 2.4-million-member Presbyterian Church (*USA*) voted 431 to 62 to start a process of phased selective divestment (*sell-off*) in multinational corporations operating in Israel. The Church manages a set of investment funds totaling approximately $7 billion USD. They too were hitting Israel economically.

The Assemblies of God: Over the years they have taken an apolitical (*not interested*) stance on Israel. This flies in the face of Scripture. (Genesis 12:3) They say, "Though we have emotional ties and affections with Israel, we cannot endorse and approve every action." On the one hand the A.O.G. say they are apolitical on the issue and then offer disapproval.

The Baptists: Articles in the Baptist Union of Great Britain publications demonstrate clearly a strongly anti-Israel and pro-Palestinian position that is derived from Christian Aid. They got together with Christian Aid and the World Council of Churches to formulate their position. We all know what a scripturally obsolete group the World Council of Churches is!

Closer to home! The Church of Vancouver reports that at the Third Lausanne Congress on World Evangelization in Cape Town showed almost half (*49 percent*) of the attending leaders sympathized with Israel and Palestine equally, while only 34 percent sympathized with Israel alone. These are the world's leading Charismatic voices, who are supposed to be

18

committed to global evangelism. They also include some who claim to walk in what they call renewal. The very ones who should be getting on board with what the LORD is doing in our day either oppose Him or remain non-committal.

The battle lines between God and Satan are clearly drawn. Churches openly come against the work of the Lord in our day! Churches using the almighty dollar, economics, to halt the work of the King of prosperity! Churches that just don't want to be bothered! While even others, so busy with the doctrinal error that is prevalent in the House of God today, have no time for the Jew. Why are so many things around us far more important than the Lord's children missing in a world of darkness and despair?

Only Jesus can sort out this mess! Only He, by supernatural intervention can reveal where His children are and bring them home. He is obviously not going to get much help from the church of our day. We were devoured by the wiles of the devil with many delusions. (Ephesians 6:11) Subterfuges that we're promised would be with us through the end times. (Matthew 24:24) Only through the supernatural intervention of the Lord, can the church be brought back from the brink. Where we are going and the conclusion of our journey should help us understand how the enemy works and how Jesus will overcome in the end.

As the search for the missing tribes raged on, many doctrines took to the church stage. Doctrines that have come down throughout the years and where fragments of error remain in many churches even today. Errors that form a pattern and part of a greater plan designed by hell for our time. The enemy works by infiltrating the church here a little, there a little, over the years. With each step he carries believers, one step at a time, further and further away from, "the whole counsel of God." Then too, some of his games he designs for detection by alert church leaders so that other aspects of his plan go undetected. The more he infiltrates the church, the easier it becomes for believers to buy into another error. When discovered, it sometimes takes generations to remove the embedded wrong. Since, fragments remain, it opens the door for the later introduction of more error. Evils that are particularly tuned for our day, to bewilder people, at the point of their need. Together, let's travel back in time to one of his earlier deceptions and discover its fragments today!

Richard Brothers (*Canadian*) was the true founder of the Anglo-Israelism Movement when he wrote: A Revealed Knowledge of the Prophecies and Times in 1794 AD.

Brothers, (*1757-1824*) was a religious fanatic and ex-naval officer, born in Newfoundland, Canada. He announced himself in 1793 as, "the nephew of the Almighty" and the apostle of his new religion. In 1795, he prophesied the destruction and end of the British monarchy. The authorities immediately dispatched him to Newcastle in the North Country of England and afterwards to an asylum from 1795-1806. Despite this, and the failure of his earlier prophecy, he declared that Jerusalem would be restored to the Jews in 1798. Even with his track record of error, his movement flourished. By the end of the nineteenth century, they boasted two million adherents of British or Anglo-Israelism, most of them were Church of England members.

Let's take a brief look at what these deceived people believe. They say that history records that Israel broke covenant with the Lord and as a result, they were all scattered and lost their covenant with the LORD. A Scripture often used to support their assumptions:

"Therefore the LORD was very angry with Israel, and removed them out of his sight: there was none left but the tribe of Judah only." (2 Kings 17:18)

At first glance, this statement in Scripture might indeed seem to indicate that no one was left except the tribe of Judah. It's a classic example of what happens when someone picks out a single verse, as a means to an end. They say that when scattered, many made their way into Africa, Europe and eventually to the British Isles. Their Scriptural foundation for their claim is:

"Listen, O isles, unto me; and hearken, ye people, from far; The LORD hath called me from the womb; from the bowels of my mother hath he made mention of my name." (Isaiah 49:1)

They also insist that Jeremiah spoke of the missing tribes being gathered from the British Isles.

"Hear the word of the LORD, O ye nations, and declare it in the isles afar off, and say, He that scattered Israel will gather him, and keep him, as a shepherd doth his flock." (Jeremiah 31:10)

In the process of this, somehow they came up with a replacement theology with a difference. Replacement, which is racing through the churches today, is the belief that the covenant was taken from Israel and given to the church. What Anglo-Israelism teaches is that; "because the missing tribes went to the British Isles, Canada and the United States, through immigration, Anglophones now hold covenant with the LORD"!

In the process of time this error was further extended by the cultist, Herbert W. Armstrong, of the Worldwide Church of God. Armstrong contended that the modern throne of England is an extension of David's throne, and that the "Stone of Scone," upon which the queen was crowned, actually was the pillar of Jacob. (Genesis 28:11)

The "stone of scone" was historically placed under the throne. It came from Scotland, not Israel, and was returned there in recent years. Many believers of Anglo-Israelism actually believe that when Jesus returns, He will sit on the throne of England. This nonsense had the higher echelons of the Church of England hoodwinked.

It's said that when a monarch is crowned, as the crown is placed on his/her head they are given instructions. "This crown is given to you for a time, then when the King of kings comes you must cast it at His feet and declare that He alone is worthy." (Revelation 5:12) Whether or not this is a result of Anglo-Israelism is unknown; however, it is worthy of note. The advancement of their replacement ideas also found a way into the Mormon belief structure. Another cult!

The Mormons teach a similarly absurd doctrine. In Mormon lore, it's alleged that in 600 B.C., during the reign of King Zedekiah, a man named Lehi, together with a companion, Ishmael, left Jerusalem and sailed to America. It's argued that Mulek, Zedekiah's son, joined Lehi, and the two groups combined to form a great nation. Mormons claim that these people were the ancestors of the American Indians. In Joseph Smith's "Articles of Faith," it states:

"We believe in the literal gathering of Israel and in the restoration of the Ten Tribes; that Zion (*the New*

Jerusalem) will be built on the American continent; that Christ will reign personally on the earth; and that the earth will be renewed and receive its paradisiacal glory."
- Article 10

Wow! He is now headed for Salt Lake City. (*Their Zion*) The Mount of Olives gets no mention. The old expression comes to mind. "Birds of a feather flock together."

Now let's look at the truth of the Word of God. Every doctrinal error comes about by people who neglect the whole counsel of God. (Acts 20:27) They pick pieces from here or there to suit their own deluded ideas. Let's go hunting for what to man are the missing tribes of Israel.

The end of the northern Kingdom did not mean an end to the ten tribes, as a brief review of Israel's history will show. In the ninth year of Hoshea's reign, (*Last King of Israel*) the people of Israel were exiled to Assyria. (2 Kings 17:6) This corresponds to the sixth year of the reign of Judah's King Hezekiah. (2 Kings 18:9-11) Hezekiah was then followed by Manasseh, (2 Kings 20:2) Amon (2 Kings 21:19) and Josiah. (2 Kings 21:24)

Beginning in the twelfth year of Josiah's reign, the Bible records the following:

"And he, (*Josiah*) burnt the bones of the priests upon their altars, and cleansed Judah and Jerusalem.

And so did he in the cities of Manasseh, and Ephraim, and Simeon, even unto Naphtali, with their mattocks round about.

And when he had broken down the altars and the groves, and had beaten the graven images into powder, and cut down all the idols throughout all the land of Israel, he returned to Jerusalem.

23

Now in the eighteenth year of his reign, when he had purged the land, and the house, he sent Shaphan the son of Azaliah, and Maaseiah the governor of the city, and Joah the son of Joahaz the recorder, to repair the house of the LORD his God.

And when they came to Hilkiah the high priest, they delivered the money that was brought into the house of God, which the Levites that kept the doors had gathered of the hand of Manasseh and Ephraim, and of all the remnant of Israel, and of all Judah and Benjamin; and they returned to Jerusalem." (2 Chronicles 34: 5-9)

It's abundantly clear, from this passage that Judah was not alone at home. Here, more than ninety years after the fall of the northern Kingdom, the Levites were able to collect money from Manasseh, Ephraim and the remnant of Israel.

King Josiah who was determined to keep the Passover as it should be kept is recorded in 2 Chronicles 35:18:

"Neither did all the kings of Israel keep such a Passover as Josiah kept, and the priests, and the Levites, and all Judah and Israel that were present, and the inhabitants of Jerusalem."

Evidently, then Judah was not alone in keeping the Passover either. People from the northern Kingdom kept it as well. Historical records from that time also show that many of the ten tribes remained in the land. I guess they are not so missing after all. Is this why only 785 genetically approved Jews went home from Ireland to the Promised Land?

Over the years, this doctrine has invaded many groups. Who they are will surprise you. As time passed, they schemed and manipulated their way even into Pentecostal circles.

The Revival Centers International, a well-known, full-bore, Pentecostal group, for some time, in hidden fashion, taught British-Israelism. Based in Melbourne, Australia, their website still today, under "Plan and Prophecy," displays a full image of the throne of England. They have stated: "We believe the Bible identifies the Anglo-Saxon-Celtic people with the nation Israel." (Wikipedia)

Even though on the outside they claim to no longer teach this error, the very presence of the throne of England may indicate that it continues on a deeper level. Revival Centers International in Australia is one of the so-called renewal mega-churches which holds influence over many others. So how did it get into Pentecostalism?

Charles Fox Parham, (1873–1929) the great American preacher, was instrumental in the formation of Pentecostalism. He was an adherent. He was also a regular speaker at "the Azusa Street Outpouring." The enemy gets on the inside of revivals and today's so-called renewals to spread his lies. Since it comes from respected men and women known in renewal, it's believed verbatim.

In 1948, a revival began in an independent Pentecostal Bible school in Saskatchewan, Canada. (*The Latter Rain Movement*). This movement led by George and Ernest Hawtin and Percy Hunt, former leaders in the Pentecostal Assemblies of Canada (*the Assemblies of God counterpart in Canada*). Hawtin's school began displaying many of the practices common in early Pentecostal Bible schools. While the movement was disowned by the major North American Pentecostal

25

denominations, it had an immense impact on the post-war Pentecostal healing revivals and the later development of the charismatic movement.

George Hawtin published his British-Israel doctrines in his periodical, "The Page," and later in book form as a series of articles. Determined to push through his ideas within Pentecostal circles, he set about trying to "prove" the identity of the Anglo-Saxon people. By a process of elimination based on thirteen "marks of identification," only one group fit their description as outlined in his interpretation of Scripture. He would have fit well into Hitler's Nazi Germany as he searched for a pure Arian race.

In his day, Britain was truly great in the eyes of the world. Thus, he cited Genesis 12:2.

"And I will make of thee a great nation, and I will bless thee, and make thy name great; and thou shalt be a blessing."

Hawtin said, "This was fulfilled only in the name of Great Britain." "Israel, Britain," he said, "was exceedingly fruitful and very populous and shall rule over many nations, but none shall rule over her." Hawtin, writing after 1967, reassessed biblical prophecy in light of the new political situation then facing Great Britain.

"In Ephesians 2:12, Paul speaks of Israel as a commonwealth," wrote Hawtin. Great Britain had gone from being an empire to a Commonwealth of Nations. "In fact, the changing global political map was all part of God's plan," he said. "The crumbling of the British Empire, together with the dreadful weakening of the power of the Unites States of America, is definitely foretold in Scripture and is one of the principal signs that

26

we are at the end of the age when all things shall be finished."

His teachings swept through the Assemblies of God and the Pentecostal Assemblies of Canada. This in turn affected many other church groups.

The Revival Centers International, members of the Assemblies of God, did their damage. Of course, the incubator of error, Bethel Church in Redding, California, who promote many erroneous teachings were part of the A.O.G. On January 17th, 2006, they voted to withdraw from their affiliation. This, they did in an unceremonious way and contrary to the bylaws of the constitution of the organization to which they ascribed. Their departure had nothing to do with Anglo-Israelism; many fragmented ideas of it still remained in their ranks.

Through print media, Destiny Publishers in the United States continues to pump out this doctrine into the hearts of the innocent. From Sherbourne Street in Toronto, the British-Israel-World Federation use regular Podcasts, to pump this stuff out to the world. Primarily, they still teach that the Anglo-Celtic-Saxon people are the present-day physical descendants of ancient Israel, the kingdom of ten tribes, spoken of in the Bible.

All around us from many directions, doctrines of demons expounded cause immense damage. British-Israelism is only one! Since fragments lingered, more error has come in our day! Every remaining splinter is being built on as part of the grand plan and purpose of Satan.

UNDERSTANDING PRESENCE

Despite the ocean of preachers calling people not to limit what God can do, many themselves do that very thing. As never before, the Master is calling us to move in dimensions of power that we have never dreamed possible. Of course, the enemy has pulled out all the stops to distract us from that blessing.

As we race towards the last great finale of the church on the earth, we talk about a faith that moves mountains, but never do it. Many call themselves prophets, but they never physically step beyond the boundaries of time and into the great beyond. John did so on the Island of Patmos. (Revelation 4) Ezekiel did, when he measured the temples. (Ezekiel 40-48) Jesus said the things we saw Him do, we are to do also, and even greater things can we do! Where are they? (John 14:12) Everything around us today, every teaching we receive, simply limits us more and keeps us from walking in the great and mighty things we know nothing about. (Jeremiah 33:3)

It's time for a change! No more so-called manifestations that are only a drop in the bucket compared to what is in the Bible. No more counterfeits! No more half measures! It's time for the church to rise up from our long slumber. If need be, it's time for a non-violent revolution within the body! It's time to put a demand on church leadership, to believe God for the real and reject the watered down Word meant to suit the crowd. It's time, once more, to test the spirits to see if they actually line up with God's Word.

"Beloved, believe not every spirit, but try the spirits whether they are of God: because many false prophets are gone out into the world." (1 John 4:1)

In our day, this Scripture is vital for our very survival. All agree that we are living in the last days. Jesus told us that lying signs and wonders would run rampant, in our day.

"For there shall arise false Christs, and false prophets, and shall shew great signs and wonders; insomuch that, if it were possible, they shall deceive the very elect." (Matthew 24:24)

Notice the connection between the words of Jesus in John and those of Matthew. "False Prophets," they are the authors of deception.

The days of true prophecy, seeing beyond, is coming back to the church. However, today in many churches, so-called prophets offer people what to them is some inner impression and not something based in fact and experienced by the seer. Today, "prophetic words" are general and non-predictive enough that they are impossible to confirm or deny.

Some so-called prophets, who are slightly specific are right only one out of six times. With such errors, these words need confirmation one way or the other. When they have been wrong in the past and then bring another prophecy, the discerning will wonder. Even so, they may not risk sounding less spiritual by raising questions of why hearers should believe their words. Dejectedly, when they hear God's Word preached, they may also doubt that too since no clear distinction between the words of the Prophet Jeremiah and the words of the prophet John Doe are present. Both had a gift and calling to speak God's words, but did they?

29

All this has come about by a watered down church. People are backward to stand up and speak up! We feel that those in the pulpit know more than we who listen. During the week we are too busy with so many things. There was no time to study the Word to see, if what people teach lines up with the Word. Here, lies the heart of the problem. Tolerated error had been brought forth in the history of the church, we learned to accept it then and it's happening again!

We cannot have it both ways. Either John Doe is bringing words from God as the biblical prophets did, or he is not. If he claims to speak with God's authority like a prophet of old and his words do not prove correct, by Old Testament Law, the person required stoning, (Deuteronomy 18:20) or at the very least, in our "age of grace," discredited and no longer trusted to bring prophetic words. Presumably, he would be encouraged to stay seated and not stand and speak for God because he has a history of misunderstanding or misrepresenting Scripture. This is why we need to test the spirits to see if they are of God.

Many are very kindly people who themselves are deceived. However, until real prophets, until the real everything, finds restoration in the church, we need to take some things with a grain of salt.

The same kind of error touches many of the teachings in the church today. Let's look at a few, starting with The Presence of the Lord or the Glory Cloud.

Some false prophets tell people there are seven key ways to sense God's Presence. The word sensitivity tells the story. In the Bible, The Presence of the Lord or the Glory Cloud were physical manifestations and not something sensed.

Some expositors tell people that "to experience His presence we have to come clean with Him." To define that, they say: "Sometimes you can't sense God's presence because there's something blocking the communication between the two of you."

Next they tell us to read Scripture aloud. To this, they say: "When you audibly speak God's inspired Word, you will sense its power and His presence." Notice the "*its*," they cannot even personify The Presence of the Lord. It's the LORD, and not a book that has the power!

They then go on to say, sing Him a love song. For this they explain: "When you start praising Him, regardless of where you are, you'll sense His presence."

Further, they want us to say His name. "Say His name aloud – as the answer to all you seek, as the Source to calm your soul."

The next one confused me. "Say a Breath Prayer."

I had never heard that expression before they gave the details. "I need you. The simplest of cries are the ones that penetrate His heart the quickest."

Next, they stretch themselves way beyond the truth of Scripture. They say that to experience His presence, the Shekinah, take a walk. They say: "Exercise brings your body, mind and heart to life." This is from a well-known ministry in Redding California! It's Bethel Church, mentioned earlier.

Then, they want us to breathe deeply. They claim: "Sometimes we can't sense God's presence because there's too much of everything else going on. Too much noise. Too much traffic. Too much confusion. Too many thoughts running rampant in our minds. Too much anxiety. Center your mind on Him and start to breathe deeply."

It all sounds like they are saying that the LORD is some far away God who is difficult to reach. The Psalmist said:

"Where shall I go from your Spirit? Or where shall I flee from your presence?" (Psalm 139:7 ESV)

Besides that, everywhere in both the Old and New Testaments, His presence was physical and tangible. Let's apply the test of Scripture to each of these seven steps. Can comparisons be found in the Word of God, giving us a pattern of how to experience the Presence or Glory Cloud? If it's not in the Word, toss it out the door along with the expositors!

"Come clean with Him. Sometimes you can't sense God's presence because there's something blocking the communication between the two of you."

The Children of Israel, had just come out of Egypt. (Exodus 12:51) Egyptian mentality filled them. The LORD had brought them out of Egypt, then He had to get Egypt out of them. In short, they were filthy and in need of spiritual cleansing. That cleansing did not come3 until sometime later:

"And the LORD said unto Moses, Go unto the people, and sanctify them today and tomorrow, and let them wash their clothes." (Exodus 19:10.)

Their spiritual condition had nothing to do with any appearance of The Presence of the Lord. The cloud appeared back in Exodus 13:21, long before the cleansing of Exodus 19.

"And the LORD went before them by day in a pillar of a cloud, to lead them the way; and by night in a pillar of fire, to give them light; to go by day and night." (Exodus 13:21)

"Read Scripture aloud. When you audibly speak God's inspired Word, you will sense its power and His presence." There is that "*its*," again.

During the exodus, the spoken word was all they had until the day the commandments were given in Exodus 20. It wasn't until later that Moses wrote the Pentateuch, the first five books of the Bible. In fact, Scripture records the first time the book of Moses was read, as mentioned in Nehemiah.

"On that day they read in the book of Moses in the audience of the people; and therein was found written." Nehemiah 13:1a)

So obviously, reading the Word aloud had nothing to do with His presence.

"Sing Him a love song. When you start praising Him, regardless of where you are, you'll sense His presence."

The first time anyone sang a love song to the LORD was Moses and it happened long after the cloud of His presence appeared.

"Then sang Moses and the children of Israel this song unto the LORD, and spake, saying, I will sing unto the LORD, for he hath triumphed gloriously: the horse and his rider hath he thrown into the sea." (Exodus 15:1)

Thus, singing had nothing to do with experiencing His presence either.

The next one was... "Say His name aloud, as the answer to, all you seek, as the Source to calm your soul."

No one was singing or saying His name when the cloud of His presence first appeared. The Bible does not say they called on the name of the LORD there! They were on the run to get out of Egypt and away from their slave masters. During his song in Exodus 15:3, Moses did mention the name of the LORD, not to invoke, but to praise. The Glory Cloud, Jesus, was already manifest.

"Say a Breath Prayer. I need you. The simplest of cries are the ones that penetrate His heart the quickest."

Although their reasoning of what they call a breath prayer is sound, its context is far from Scripture and common sense when it comes to The Presence of the Lord. The Cloud of His presence, as such, was never invoked or initiated by man. It was initiated by God. (Exodus 13:21-22)

"Take a walk. Exercise brings your body, mind and heart to life." Can you show me one single Scripture that says that God's presence was ever invoked by taking a walk? Yes, Israel was taking a walk, a very long walk, but not to invoke anything. Their walk was in obedience as they escaped from the hands of brutal taskmasters.

"Breathe deeply. Sometimes we can't sense God's presence because there's too much of everything else going on. Too much noise. Too much traffic. Too much confusion. Too many thoughts running rampant in our minds. Too much anxiety."

At the crossing of the Red Sea, (Exodus 14) the people were afraid. Their emotions ran rampant. They shouted. All sorts of noises were present. There were over one million on the move with carts. There was a noise of traffic, perhaps greater than what we know about on the drive to work. The sounds of advancing Egyptian chariots added to their emotions. Would they make it across the river before the Egyptians overtook them? Anxiety would have screamed. Would the river stay open or will some die in the crossing? The manifestation of the Presence of the Lord was not hindered, delayed or diminished in intensity by any of this! The Presence of the Lord was a physical and tangible manifestation, experienced not through their senses. Rather, they saw Him, felt Him, knew His guidance and experienced the benefit of light and warmth at nighttime. (Exodus 13:21)

Just about every church I know, in their doctrinal statement, holds that Scripture is the final authority. If they truly believe that is the case, then every manifestation of His presence must line up with and be discoverable in the Bible. In fact, the church in Redding, California, has this in their doctrinal statement.

"The Bible is the inspired and only infallible and authoritative Word of God." I guess they set that aside when they wrote their Seven Steps to Experience God's Presence!

What is happening today is that the enemy has us basing things on what we experience, and not the truth of the Word. Let's see if we can understand the depth of the problem!

When trying to measure time or weight or temperature or speed or any of a hundred other things, we make a huge leap forward when we stop trusting our senses or intuition and start relying on instrumentation (*The Bible*). For instance, trying to tell the time by using our feelings, such as how hungry or tired we feel by our senses are crudely inaccurate compared to using an empirical measure of a clock! Likewise, guessing from circumstances or whether we feel guilty or happy or peaceful or excited or blessed, is a most unreliable way of gauging spiritual reality.

The more important a matter is, the more critical it is that we stop going by what we sense and start relying on an objective measure (*The Bible*). What if an airline pilot ignored the plane's instrumentation and decided to fly by his gut feeling?

Spiritual matters are literally more important than life and death. All of eternity hinges on them. The stakes are far too high to rely on our feelings or circumstances to guess spiritual reality. We need the Word of God as our ultimate instrumentation and final authority. If it's not in the Word, be more than careful!

Sensations like feeling God's presence are so vague as to be virtually useless as a spiritual gauge. To base one's faith on such feelings would be a disaster for anyone. One's faith is found in God's integrity and His Word.

Do not rely on our own understanding, warns Scripture. (Proverbs 3:5) There is a way that seems right, but it leads to death, screams another verse. (Proverbs 14:12) The precision, of God's Word is vital. Each revelation of Scripture is like dials in a pilot's cockpit. Give more credence to our gut feeling than to one of them, and our spiritual life is on the line.

The Bible affirms that a prophet can speak in the name of God and his prophecies can be supernaturally accurate and yet if his message does not align with Scripture, their theology, their words, deserve utter rejection! (Deuteronomy 13:1-4)

If the great apostle Paul, who worked miracles in the name of Christ, proclaimed a gospel different to that recorded in Scripture, his words must be rejected. The same, he insisted, applied to a message from an angel. (Galatians 1:8) Even the darkest force in all creation can appear as an angel of light. (2 Corinthians 11:14)

The Deceiver can give us a false spiritual experience, but he cannot change the Bible. "Heaven and earth will pass away," said Jesus, "but my word will never pass away." (Matthew 24:35)

Once more, we are in a time of fervor for the things of God! In the past, the enemy introduced his error during such times. He is doing it again!

"Ye shall not add unto the word which I command you, neither shall ye diminish ought from it, that ye may keep the commandments of the LORD your God which I command you." (Deuteronomy 4:2)

In our day, diminishment and additions are rampant in the circus of wrong doctrine.

If we claim that Jesus is the same yesterday, today and forever, (Hebrews 13:8) applying this to a multitude of experiences around today, then those words must apply to all manifestations. Even when it comes to the presence of the Living God, in what many today claim as the attendance of a cloud of glory in meetings, the same rule must apply! Take warning, the deceptions of the enemy are running rampant!

THE GLORY CLOUD

What is the Glory Cloud? The answer to this question can only be found in the pages of our final authority and not in the realm of the senses of man.

The cloud of God's presence! (*The Shekinah*) Actually, no such word as Shekinah is found in Scripture. Another descriptive word occurs for the first time in the Exodus account, (13:21) although some would trace it back to the rainbow "in the cloud" in Genesis 9:13-16. God was presented to the Children of Israel during the exodus as a pillar of cloud by day, (*cloudy pillar*) and a fiery pillar by night. Moses went up on the mountain where "the glory of the Lord settled on Mount Sinai, and the cloud covered it for six days." (Exodus 24:16)

If interpreted in poetic Hebrew parallelism, one realizes that "the glory of the Lord" and "the cloud" are synonymous. Each is simply an amplification, a reiteration, of the other. The cloud represents the presence of God. Note that God called to Moses out of the cloud, (Exodus 24:16) descended as a cloud, (*in a cloud*) on the Tabernacle where Moses was. (Exodus 33:9) Then, from the cloud God spoke to Moses when he went up a second time for the stone tablets. (Exodus 34:5) Scripture says that Moses's face glowed and that people could see that glow after he had been in the cloud, in the presence of God.

Other places in Scripture also refer to the presence of God as a cloud. When Isaiah had his vision in the temple, suddenly the room was full of a "fiery cloud" or smoke, (Isaiah 6:4) a reference to the perceived glory of God. Ezekiel, speaking of the indescribable glory of God, refers to a cloud, (Ezekiel 1:4) and ends by saying that his description of God's glory was threefold. What he described was not God, or even the glory of God, but only "the appearance of the likeness of the glory of the Lord." (Ezekiel 1:28) God's glory is beyond words!

Paul speaks of the people of Israel being under the cloud, all of them being baptized in the cloud and in the sea. (1 Corinthians 10:1-2) At the end of time, Paul says, we will be caught up in the cloud and will be forever in the presence of God. (1 Thessalonians 4:17) Again the cloud and the presence of God are together.

The gospel writers seem particularly interested in helping their readers focus on the transfiguration and ascension. With the aid of a Strong's Exhaustive Concordance we get a clear picture of both.

On the mountain were Jesus, Peter, James and John. Suddenly a brilliant metamorphosis began to take place which would be completed at the ascension. His face radiated with a brilliance. Even His clothes became luminous with firelight. Then, a bright cloud overshadowed the four of them. They describe this as glorious with transparent light, and they knew it was totally supernatural.

Leaping forward to the ascension we discover a wonderful conclusion to the metamorphosis that began at the Transfiguration.

"When he had spoken these things, while they beheld, he was taken up; and a cloud received him out of their sight.

And while they looked steadfastly toward heaven as he went up, behold, two men stood by them in white apparel;

Which also said, ye men of Galilee, why stand ye gazing up into heaven? This same Jesus, which is taken up from you into heaven, shall so come in like manner as ye have seen him go into heaven." (Acts 1:9-11)

The ascension was a glorious event. Our Lord disappeared into a cloud, not into "the clouds." It was the same cloud that was present at the Transfiguration.

Nothing is any clearer than this description of the glory cloud at the transfiguration. Not only were there miraculous appearances present, all who were there, including Moses and Elijah, entered into conversation with each other. Here is what we should expect when the glory cloud appears in our meetings.

During the past number of years some churches began to report the appearance of a "glory cloud." In particular, Bethel Church in Redding, California has been at its center. There are no greater expositors of error than those at Bethel. They believe this to be a physical manifestation of God's presence in the form of a glittery cloud that lingers over worship services. Such clouds have now been reported in services all over the world, from one-room house churches to mega-churches.

Those who have witnessed this phenomenon describe it as a glittering swarm of gold-like particles that settles on skin and hair and then vanishes upward. Some describe hands and faces covered in a glittery residue that returns even after wiping it off. There are also reports of feathers or "jewels" falling from these clouds. Even others speak of the appearance of gold teeth. Some pastors, claim that the cloud has so enveloped them before preaching that they could hardly see the congregation. They attribute it to the tangible presence of God, anointing them for preaching. They use as their biblical foundation Old Testament passages such as 2 Chronicles 5:14; 1 Kings 8:11; Ezekiel 10:4; Isaiah 60:1-2 and Exodus 40:35.

Before we look at the Scriptures that they use as their biblical foundation for this manifestation, let's look at the idea that it disappears and wipes off. They claim these things are a special gift from God in our day; however, they disappear upwards. Consider this verse:

"For the gifts and calling of God are without repentance." (Romans 11:29)

The Pulpit Commentary says of this verse:

"For the gifts χαρίσματα, meaning 'free gifts,' or 'gifts of grace;' the word used to denote the special gifts of the Holy Ghost that God, of his own good will, grants freely and the calling of God are without repentance."

If the appearance of glitter is a special gift from God, then why does it disappear? Did God take it back? Further, if it's a gift of God, why would they try to wipe it off?

Now let's read the Scriptures that many quote as their biblical foundation indicating support for their manifestation theology!

"So that the priests could not stand to minister by reason of the cloud: for the glory of the LORD had filled the house of God." (2 Chronicles 5:14)

No commentator, no Hebrew transliteration of any word in this verse speaks of glitter descending! Nor does it say that a speaker, anointed to preach, could not see the congregation as they preached. It says they could not minister! The preachers of this error claim it is part of a new anointing! The second passage, they offer and similar to the first is:

"So that the priests could not stand to minister because of the cloud: for the glory of the LORD had filled the house of the LORD." (1 Kings 8:11)

Here, the word "filled" translates out to mean that the house was bursting at the seams with the Glory Cloud. Once more, nothing about glitter is mentioned!

He filled the temple with His glory! Nothing indicates that His appearance occurred in just one part of the building. The glitter cloud, in some churches, no matter what the color, appears in only one part of the church or another. Of course, this is part of what they call a new anointing when in fact the Cannon of Scripture is closed. (Revelation 23:18-19) Following their given Scriptures as their biblical base for this foundation we come to:

"The house was filled with the cloud, and the court was full of the brightness of the LORD'S glory." (Ezekiel 10:4b)

Here, everyone in the building saw and experienced the manifestation, not just a few. Why are not all in the affected churches today experiencing it? They say it's because not all in the building are walking in the new anointing! Here is another quote from one experienced pundit.

"The gold dust appearing helps remind us of the spiritual truth that God is majestic and rich in spiritual blessings. We know God is with us and when the gold dust manifests itself, this truth is confirmed and our hearts soar in praise of our Royal King who created the universe and can create gold dust, gems, oil, or any other thing he wishes to give us a glimpse of his power and greatness."

Did you catch that? "When the gold dust manifests itself." She is saying that this is a self-creating manifestation. This glitter, she infers, has the power to appear and disappear. Her words also suggest that if someone does not experience it, then God is not with them. To justify her position on the glitter, she says:

"The Prophet Isaiah prophesied the following words. 'For behold, darkness will cover the earth and deep darkness the people; But the LORD will rise upon you and His glory will appear upon you.'" (Isaiah 60:2)

Her implication is that the prophet meant that so-called gold dust would be the covering! You decide! Doctrine, real or imagined?

The last Scripture they use is also found in Exodus.

"And Moses was not able to enter into the tent of the congregation, because the cloud abode thereon, and the glory of the LORD filled the tabernacle." (Exodus 40:35)

Here, the preacher could not even get into the church. The manifestation was so strong, so powerful, it was the real Presence of the Lord.

Those who met the cloud of God's glory in the Old Testament were often unable to approach Him. (Exodus 40:34–35; 2 Chronicles 7:2; and 1 Kings 8:11) By contrast, those experiencing the modern version of "a glory cloud" greet it with singing, dancing, shouting, and basking in the glitter that engulfs them. This response is inconsistent with biblical accounts. When the glory of God was present in a cloud, the power of His presence was so overwhelming that mortal men could not enter it.

Although the Lord God can manifest any way He chooses to, He does not need a cloud or specks of glitter to communicate His presence to those who have received His offer of salvation by faith. These folks that chase a manifestation do not realize that it's not something new. The leaders of these movements fell afoul to this by the hands of others. Who are they?

There is also mention of another cloud in the Bible.

"Which have forsaken the right way, and are gone astray, following the way of Balaam the son of Bosor, who loved the wages of unrighteousness;

But was rebuked for his iniquity: the dumb ass speaking with man's voice forbad the madness of the prophet.

These are wells without water, clouds that are carried with a tempest; to whom the mist of darkness is reserved for ever.

For when they speak great swelling words of vanity, they allure through the lusts of the flesh, through much wantonness, those that were clean escaped from them who live in error.

While they promise them liberty, they themselves are the servants of corruption: for of whom a man is overcome, of the same is he brought in bondage." (2 Peter 2:15-19)

The first thing we need to notice is that "other cloud." These verses describe those who speak great swelling words that promote spiritual adultery. Their goal: crowds and full offering plates. The name Balaam, in Strong's is: (G903) "Βαλαάμ – Balaam - bal-ah-am. Of Hebrew origin symbolic of a false teacher."

Peter warned against "the way of Balaam," Jude against the error of Balaam and John against the doctrine of Balaam. (2 Peter 2:15, Jude 11, Revelation 2:14) God evidently considers these warnings necessary and appropriate for Christians even today.

Yet Balaam, for a time in his day, was a genuine prophet, (2 Peter 2:16) possessed great knowledge concerning God, and even received direct revelations from God. What, therefore, was his way, his error, and his doctrine?

"The way of Balaam" was a readiness to prostitute his higher spiritual gifts and privileges for the wages of unrighteousness. (2 Peter 2:14) Being willing to preach

44

something contrary to God's Word for personal gain or recognition. Something that was contrary to our final authority.

The error of Balaam was evidently his willingness to compromise his own standards of morality and truth in order to greedily accommodate those who were his pagan listeners. (Jude 11)

Finally, the doctrine of Balaam! Even in John's day it was already infiltrating the church. He used his teaching authority to persuade God's people that it was all right for them to compromise the standards of the final authority and have them accept less than the full manifestation of the Lord. These use spiritual tyranny to achieve their goals. Spiritual adultery (Revelation 2:14) with their idol-worshipping enemies.

No wonder Micah (*the faithful prophet*) urged God's people to "remember" Balaam and his tragic end. (Micah 6:5, Numbers 31:8)

If Balaam lived among today's evangelicals, he would be considered a great man. His public proclamations would be widely known, and his "ministry" would have great impact. (Numbers 22:6) In his day, Balaam was also known for his "prayer power." That is, when he spoke to the Lord, Balaam usually got an answer. (Numbers 22:8, 18) He certainly would have been at home among many of today's mega-church leaders. This is how the enemy works!

Balaam, had an appetite for monetary success and a desire for secular recognition. (2 Peter 2:15, Jude 11) He deliberately embraced error in spite of the Lord's warnings and with clear foreknowledge that he was doing wrong. (Numbers 22–24) There are many today in both pulpit and pew who know what they are doing is wrong! They search the word daily to find some verse out of context to justify their actions.

"But I have a few things against thee, because thou hast there them that hold the doctrine of Balaam, who taught Balac to cast a stumbling-block before the children of Israel, to eat things sacrificed unto idols, and to commit fornication." (Revelation 2:14)

When we are taught anything that does not line up entirely with the final authority, the Bible, great caution needs to be exercised. Has a stumbling block been set in our way?

A number of years ago, I was ministering in a church in England. The atmosphere was electric as the Word was preached. In the midst of the sermon my attention was arrested by a man sitting in a wheelchair. He had been bound in that chair for five years after experiencing a severe stroke. I stopped preaching and looked directly at the man. I commanded him in the name of Jesus to rise and walk. In an instant he was out of the chair and started to run up and down in the church. People cheered and shouted praises to the King saying, "He is the same yesterday, today and forever."

Later I learned that his daughter had sat quietly in the meeting. After the service I engaged her in conversation.

"What do you think of what the Lord did for your dad?" Her answer floored me!

"That was OK, but does the Lord give gold teeth through your ministry?" Instantly I knew what spirit she was of! The manifestation of so-called gold was more important than the one who manifested grace!

Who is he that wants us to settle for less than the absolute power of God manifested? For years preachers have told us not to settle for less than the Lord's best! Yet, why is it now, they want us to settle for a few specks of glitter when reality demands buildings on fire with His glory? Churches so filled with the glory cloud that people cannot get in the door? Communications, loud and audible from within the cloud of His presence? Where are the glowing faces, so bright that the people become afraid? So much so that we have to put a bag over our head?

It almost seems like we live in times when people everywhere are crying out for a sign.

"And he sighed deeply in his spirit, and saith, why doth this generation seek after a sign? Verily I say unto you, There shall no sign be given unto this generation." (Mark 8:12)

It's time for a revolution in the church where we demand the real! Where by every peaceful means, we bring about an end to easy-believism. Where we find the courageous love to stand up and confront error on every hand, no matter what price we shall forfeit.

If we cannot confront ourselves, those around us or the world at large, we should not stay in the pulpit. The definition of the word confront is "to stand face to face with." This is a skill, a virtue, in which all participants of the end time's church must excel. Believers, we must love enough to challenge those lost in a world of error on every occasion. If we do not, we do not love at all!

Jesus challenged them on every occasion. He offered to them scathing denunciations. Jesus accused them of hypocrisy and pretentiousness, and pronounced upon them a succession of woes (*seven in all*) culminating in this terrible, climactic statement:

47

"Therefore you are witnesses against yourselves that you are sons of those who murdered the prophets. Fill up, then, the measure of your fathers' guilt. Serpents, brood of vipers! How can you escape the condemnation of hell?" (Matthew 23:31-33)

His words, He loaded with love unblemished, love divine.

While the enemy was working among the glitter cloud enthusiasts, his attention was also being given to others. If some accepted this, they would receive more as he advanced his final plan and purpose!

SAVED, HEALED, DELIVERED

Bethel Church in Redding, California, promoters of the glitter cloud phenomena, has brought forth another preposterous assertion. Claims that have spread like wildfire around the globe. In the light of truth, Bethel appears as the incubator of error! Their lineage of error goes all the way back to the day when they were members of a group that supported Anglo-Israelism. Next came the glitter cloud, orbs of light, angel feathers and now this. They call it, "Sozo Ministry."

Naturally, they say that those who oppose their ideas are the ones deceived. Many, with extreme intensity of emotions or conviction defend them when challenged by the final authority, the Word of God. Other church leaders refuse to confront their members even while they are aware that they are taken by another gospel. These are afraid of ending up with a few more empty seats on Sunday.

The word "Sozo" is an amazing word translated into every language. It's been bandied about in our day with little or no understanding of its real meaning. We need to take a long hard look at it, in the light of Scripture. Teachers of it, "Sozo Ministry," say:

"SOZO is the Greek word translated 'saved, healed, and delivered.' Sozo Ministry is a unique inner healing and deliverance ministry aimed to get to the root of things hindering your personal connection with the Father, Son and Holy Spirit. With a healed connection, you can walk in the destiny to which you have been called.

A Sozo session is a time for the Sozo team to sit down with you and with the help of the Holy Spirit walk you through the process of freedom and wholeness. Sozo is not a counseling session, but a time of interacting with Father, Son and Holy Spirit for wholeness and pursuing of your destiny." – Bethel Sozo

Two things immediately jump from their own words. The first one is "session," which implies a series of meetings or events. The second one is their words: "with the help of the Holy Spirit." This would seem to relegate the third person of the Trinity to a secondary role. They are implying that they are the ones who carry it out and the Holy Spirit only helps.

When Jesus spoke to the woman with the issue of blood, He said: "Woman, thy faith hath made thee, Sozo." (Luke 8:48) Healed, free, delivered and whole at that very second. According to Strong's, the word "Sozo" also speaks of salvation, of wholeness, healing and of freedom. This is what that woman received the moment she by faith touched the hem of His garment. At no time has Jesus ever said that healing or salvation was a process or occurs through sessions!

The word "Sozo" is used 106 times in the New Testament. Let's look at a few of those verses in their context!

Salvation

"She shall bring forth a son, and thou shalt call his name JESUS: for he shall save (*Sozo*) his people from their sins." (Matthew 1:21)

"For after that in the wisdom of God the world by wisdom knew not God, it pleased God by the foolishness of preaching to save (*Sozo*) them that believe." (1 Corinthians 1:21)

"Wherefore he is able also to save (*Sozo*) them to the uttermost that come unto God by him, seeing he ever liveth to make intercession for them." (Hebrews 7:25)

Forgiven, Healed, and Delivered

"Sozo," was translated another fifty-three times as "saved" (*past tense*) in reference to the forgiveness of sins. However, there were also times where this same Greek word was translated as "healed."

(*Jairus*) "Besought (*Jesus*) greatly, saying, my little daughter lieth at the point of death: I pray thee, come and lay thy hands on her, that she may be healed; (*Sozo*) and she shall live." (Mark 5:23)

This word, "healed," is referring to physical healing. As the story unfolds, Jairus's daughter actually died, and Jesus raised her from the dead. (Mark 5:35–43) So in this instance, Sozo, "healed," refers to physical healing, even physical resurrection from the dead. This girl was dead! Jesus did not say that her resurrection would be a lengthy procedure requiring sessions. Come back for another session next week!

This same word that's used for both forgiveness of sins and physical healing also applies to deliverance from demons.

"They also which saw it told them by what means he that was possessed of the devils was healed." (*Sozo*) (Luke 8:36)

Commonly known as the demoniac of Gadarene, nobody could hold this man. In fact, he often broke the very chains that bound him. Jesus cast the demons out of him. Nowhere does it say that this was a process. He didn't use "Theophostic Therapy," "Theophostic Prayer Ministry" or "Sozo Ministry," as we know it, He spoke a word. The moment He spoke the demons left!

51

All three of those terms, "Theophostic Therapy," "Theophostic Prayer Ministry," "Sozo Ministry," are one and the same. They were changed from one to the other by Ed. Smith, the original founder, when the lawsuits against him piled up.

Let's press on towards truth! Another example is found in these words.

"The same heard Paul speak: who steadfastly beholding him, and perceiving that he had faith to be healed." "*Sozo.*" (Acts 14:9)

Paul beheld this crippled man, (*Lame from birth*) and perceived that he had faith to be healed (*Sozo*) and he was, the instant he abandoned himself to God. Nowhere does Scripture say that this came by session either!

In Mark's gospel, we learn the story of Bartimaeus, who sat by the roadside begging. When Jesus came His way, he began to cry out. "Son of David, have mercy on me." (Mark 10:46:52) The religious didn't take to his shouting and they tried to silence him. He answered them by shouting even louder. When Jesus came to him, He asked Bartimaeus what he wanted. Naturally, he wanted his sight! Here is what Jesus said in verse 52. "Go thy way; thy faith hath made thee whole." (*Sozo*) It happened immediately. Jesus didn't say, Bartimaeus, it's going to take some sessions, if you were to come back, with the help of the Holy Spirit, I can promise you change!

If we take a moment to consider the emotional aspects of these very few people we discover even more truth. The man who was blind spent years begging on the streets. His condition isolated him and condemned him to beg at the roadside. In those days, that was their social welfare program. Ask anyone who is on Social Assistance, find out if their experiences bring with them emotional upset. Sure, his emotions were broken, yet his healing, physical, emotional and spiritual was instant, not by session. His surrender was total and complete. He laid down his condition and everything associated with it.

The woman with the issue of blood had spent all she had on doctors and was none better. For twelve long years in poverty, she searched for someone to help her. I bet at times she felt like giving up. When Jesus healed her, that healing was also instantaneous. Physically, emotionally and spiritually, she was made whole. (*Sozo*) It happened the very moment she believed. Jesus never said to her, "you're healed but still more is to come down the road." He didn't say, "When you come back, you and I with the help of the Holy Spirit will work through the issues!"

When the Apostle Paul was used in the "Sozo" of the infirm man, he came face-to-face with much more than a physical condition. The man had been handicapped from the day he was born. Tell me that such does not bring with it many emotional issues. From personal experience I can tell you it does.

For seven years I was confined to a wheelchair. Just ask the person sitting in a wheelchair outside some building, waiting, hoping that someone will come by and open the door for them if it hurts. His connection with "Sozo" and my connection were both instant. (Acts 3-4)

Those who teach "Sozo," like Bethel, do so trying to fit God into man's experience and not man into the realities of God. For this reason, the church in many places (*not all*) is powerless and weak! Because their

53

preachers desire recognition, they develop theologies to bolster the absence of the final authority in their lives. They psychologically manipulate people into something that is far from the pattern of Scripture, and in this, they walk into the hands of the design of the enemy's desire.

Some who practice counseling may be godly Christian men and women with a genuine love for the Lord and His Word. Some are granted true revelation regarding others in accordance with the pattern of the Word. These operate in the gift of a word of knowledge. Such is a definite conviction, impression, or knowing that comes to them in a similitude (*a mental picture*) or by a Scripture quickened to them. Its supernatural insight or understanding of circumstances, situations, problems, or a body of facts by revelation; that is, without assistance by any human resource. It comes solely by divine aid, according to the Cannon of Scripture. Furthermore, the gift of a word of knowledge is revelation of the divine will and plan of God for the person and under the timing of the Lord. Then, the healing comes instantaneously as demonstrated by Jesus and not by session. This cannot be said universally for all who claim to use Theophostic Ministry.

Not every emotional problem is the result of a lie as claimed by Sozo teachers. Not every traumatic event needs to be brought up and dealt with for a person to experience the love of God and the joy of knowing Him. Some Theophostic counselors delve far too deeply into the arena of unbiblical psychology, such as repressed memory therapy. As with any form of "Christian counseling," there is a huge difference between counseling according to the whole counsel of the Bible and counseling using ungodly psychology while attaching Scripture references here and there.

Liars abound, and I include in that all those who use half-lies to justify their manipulative ways. There is no such thing as half-truths just in the same way as we cannot have half a hole or be half whole. Its surrender of all or not at all! We either speak the truth or lie; we have a hole or no hole at all. We are either whole (*Sozo*) or we are broken. (Mark 5:34) There are no half measures! It's one or the other. We are either alive or dead. We are going either to heaven or hell! There is only danger and destruction of the society that lies anywhere in between. Let's turn on the light of Scripture towards a little more of their claims and see what we can find.

They say: "The primary source of our present emotional pain is rarely caused by our present situation."

Interestingly, the first principle of Theophostic Prayer Ministry, "Sozo Ministry," concerns emotional pain. A search of the NASB, KJV, NKJV, NIV, ESV, NRSV and the RSV, (*the most prominent non-paraphrased translations*) versions of the Bible and you will not find the word "emotional" even once! "Sozo Ministry" is built on the idea that emotional pain is an evil thing from which every Christian must find deliverance. Is it really? Note: "Emotional" is a psychological term.

The closest biblical word that may describe what is now meant by "emotional pain" is "sorrow." (Romans 9:1-2) If "Sozo Ministry" means "sorrow" when using the phrase "emotional pain," then its practitioners are seeking deliverance from something that the Bible says that we will all have in this world. If they do not mean sorrow, grief or something similar found in the Bible, then "emotional pain" is not even addressed in the Bible. If it is not addressed, then Theophostic Ministry, (*Sozo*), is unbiblical at its core and must be rejected on that ground alone!

Let's assume, for the sake of argument, that "emotional pain" as used by the Sozo people is roughly the same as the biblical word "sorrow." Then, let's look at what the Bible teaches about sorrow. Paul said this:

"I am in Christ and I am telling you the truth. I am not lying. And my conscience, ruled by the Holy Spirit, agrees that what I say now is true.

"I have great sorrow and always feel much sadness for my own people." (Romans 9:1-3a ERV)

The cause of Paul's sorrow was the unconverted state of many of his Jewish brethren. Would some ministry deliver Paul from his sorrow? Clearly not! It is such a great godly sorrow that it could lead us into the heart of awakening where salvation flows like a river. The great Scottish Evangelist, John Knox, so overcome by the state of his precious nation, in prayer cried: "Give me Scotland or let me die." Like Paul, his sorrow was unbearable.

In John 16:20-22, Jesus predicted that His followers would weep and have sorrow while the world rejoices, but that this would be resolved when they see Him again. We are never promised the complete absence of sorrow until Christ returns and establishes His kingdom. We have comfort in our sorrows because we know our sins are forgiven and we know that one day we shall be with the Lord who wipes away every tear. (Revelation 21:4) So the issue addressed by "Sozo Ministry" emotional pain, is not a key issue in the Bible. It exists because we live in a fallen world, filled with many sorrows, but there is no ministry prescribed for removing it.

Sozo also teaches that: "Everything we presently know, feel, or are mentally aware of, has its roots in a first-time experience." Are they saying that the cause of all pain is a single event early in life? If this is a proven fact, then they have made an earth-shattering discovery that touches the realms of psychology, neurology, sociology, and anthropology; and all that without having conducted any controlled research in these fields. Further, what was Adam's first-time life event that caused him to sin? Up until the moment he ate the forbidden fruit, he was perfect. No issues, no trauma prior to that fateful hour.

The Bible never addresses "first-time experience" as an event that we must discover because it determines so much of what happens in the rest of our life. The Bible does say that sin and spiritual bondage to lust is the root cause of our problems:

"And you were dead in your trespasses and sins, in which you formerly walked according to the course of this world, according to the prince of the power of the air, of the spirit that is now working in the sons of disobedience. Among them, we too all formerly lived in the lusts of our flesh, indulging the desires of the flesh and of the mind, and were by nature children of wrath, even as the rest." (Ephesians 2:1-3 LITV)

Perhaps the "first-time experience" we need to consider, which is behind all that we experience, is: Adam's sin! "For as in Adam all die, so also in Christ all shall be made alive." (1 Corinthians 15:22) We were dead in sin before we had a first time experience of anything.

This "principal" of a determinative first-time experience as they describe is neither biblical nor scientific and is a claim without substance or evidence. Sin existed before pain! Sozo teachers claim that pain causes sin:

"We tend to act out the way we feel. If we act out our present pain, we will likely manifest sinful behavior." – Bethel Sozo

The Bible takes a different view. It says that we sin because of lust (*Original sin*). (James 1:14, 15) There is no reason, based on either Scripture or logic, to believe Bethel's claims. It is one thing when the shaky "science" of psychological theory tries to overturn the faith of Christians, (*as in the theories of Freud and Jung*) it is worse when an evangelical Christian seeks to overturn the clear teachings of the Bible, based on ideas pulled out of thin air. At least with the secular theorists, many Christians consider the source and do not take them seriously. This is worse. Furthermore, it is downright dangerous.

Here is a statement put out by Jim Banks, House of Healing Ministries. They call it their "Opening Client Visualization."

"Many people believe that they do not have a visual compliment to engaging god. (*Notice the small case for God*) They have been taught, or the enemy has led them to believe, that their primary, if not only, interaction with god is through his, (*Notice again the capitalization is absent on god and his*) written word, the Bible. This is typical of most folks with mainline evangelical denominational roots. In order to make the ministry time fruitful for a client, we often have to help them to 'open their spirit eyes.'

58

Many people believe that god, (*yet another small case god*) is accessible only through their minds and hence, all experience that is not absolutely logical, from their perspective, is not only not probable, but more to the point, not possible. Consequently, they have never tried any other method of interacting with him. (*Small case him demeaning the Lord*) That doesn't mean that is not another method, only that they have never entertained the idea that there is another one.

What the Sozo session leader must do is to help open their minds, hearts and spirits to another method of connecting with god. We can do this by a number of methods, principally by leading the Sozoee through a series of simple exercises to expand their repertoire of sensing, hearing, feeling and connecting with god."

Here we go again with the reliance on the senses with no mention whatsoever of faith. Notice the subtle steering away from the written Word to experiencing God through one's senses, hearing and feeling? Not to mention their misrepresentation of the Word itself! They teach people another way to connect with what they call, "god!" The Bible is clear with these words:

"No one can come to me unless the Father who sent me draws him. And I will raise him up on the last day." (John 6:44 ERV)

Hear it again! Their own words describe their mission to "open the minds, hearts and spirits of people to another method of connecting with god."

Another way to God? Jesus said: "I am the way, the truth, and the life. The only way to the Father is through me." (John 14:6 ERV)

The removal of the written Word of God, the final authority, and a seeking through sensual methods is exactly what the Sozo ministry is all about. So, what are the results? Are people being helped, healed, and made whole?

These people are big on what they call memory recovery. Currently, there are over eighty cases in the courts of the United States against certain Sozo Ministries. Other cases have included a man who lost his daughter. After the girl allegedly recovered a memory during a "Sozo Session," she accused her father of molesting her. The whole matter ended in the courts. Every possible test, lie detector, hypnosis, police investigation and a court of his peers declared him innocent. Another was a woman who lost her brother to suicide as a result of the Sozo teacher dredging up his abusive past. Sozo, is nothing more than a Theophostic form of therapy dealing with one's past, under the guise of a God encounter.

What does the Bible have to say about the past: It tells us to forget what lies behind, not to reinterpret it!

"But this one thing I do, forgetting those things which are behind, and reaching forth unto those things which are before." (Philippians 3:13)

Paul counted everything he had in his earlier life, whether it was good or bad in the eyes of man, "rubbish." (Philippians 3:8) In verse 15-17 of the same chapter, Paul tells us to follow his example in this matter. "Sozo Ministry" teaches the opposite. So, we either follow Paul's example and obey the Bible, or follow a speculative artificial theory that causes people to tempt God. The correct choice is clear.

If the church gets back to the message of total abandonment, of total surrender at Calvary, then any and all agony would be surrendered at the cross. Isaiah

53:4 says: "Surely he hath borne our griefs, and carried our sorrows." If it is surrendered, then it's gone!

All advocates of this sort of so-called ministry have done damage all around the globe. The moment false teaching breaches the walls of any ministry, it paves the way for much more to enter. Many such groups, snared by these new anointing theologies, are leading the church further away from truth and right into the heart of the enemy's plan for the end times.

It's for this reason we need to be intimately acquainted with the tenets of the Word of God! This requires us to get back to the written Word. Then, and only then, will we be able to effectively stand against the wiles of the devil. (Ephesians 6:11) The enemy's strategy for the unfolding of his end time's plan did not end there. In fact, these have only been the foundation upon which he planned to build.

A number of years ago, a man arrived at a school and promoted a form of spirit writing as a good method of hearing from the Lord. The students were told to read their Bibles then write down anything that came into their heads in a free-flowing way. When some of the kids started being honest and writing down what truthfully came into their heads, the principal of the school quickly abandoned the idea and told the class it was not biblical.

There are those today who say they are receiving messages from the Lord directly as He physically guides their hands to write. This is actually an occult technique called automatic writing that is beginning to move through the churches. The Lord never did that in Scripture. He spoke to the prophets and they wrote down what He said. He did not physically guide their hands.

"What thou seest, write in a book, and send it unto the seven churches." (Revelation 1:11) "And the LORD said unto Moses, Write thou these words: for after the tenor of these words I have made a covenant with thee and with Israel." (Exodus 34:27) "Moreover the LORD said unto me, Take thee a great roll, and write in it with a man's pen concerning Mahershalalhashbaz." (Isaiah 8:1) "Thus speaketh the LORD God of Israel, saying, Write thee all the words that I have spoken unto thee in a book." (Jeremiah 30:2) "And the LORD answered me and said, write the vision, and make it plain upon tables, that he may run that readeth it." (Habakkuk 2:2)

You might ask, "What about David?" David did say:

"All this, said David, the LORD made me understand in writing by his hand upon me, even all the works of this pattern." (1 Chronicles 28:19)

God did not force David's hand to write. The Holy Spirit came upon David and "gave him understanding" of the plans of God for the temple. This means that God spoke to David and David wrote those plans down.

This is how the LORD works! Everything He does today must be found in the pages of the Cannon of Scripture. If it's not there, it must be rejected out of hand. He never removes choice from us! He never removes control from His children! What is starting to pollute the church is the occult practice of automatic writing under the guise of some new anointing!

Automatic writing is defined as being: "writing performed without apparent intent or conscious control, especially to achieve a state of being as if of telepathic or spiritualistic origin." - Dictionary.com

The very definition should cause us to cringe. Regrettably, in some places it does not! In some churches and through certain ministries, believers have been deceived into thinking it is of the LORD!

How did it all begin? People in these so-called healing ministries began by having people journal. "Sozo" or "Theophostic Prayer Ministry," or at the beginning, "Theophostic Therapy" use it in follow up. Here is a statement from their follow-up pamphlets.

"After you have experienced a SOZO session, it is necessary to walk out more healing. You can keep the doors closed or re-close them if they get opened. You can also use the tools that were used in your session for the rest of your life to not allow the strongholds to resurface.

We encourage you to journal or tell someone what happened during your SOZO. Journaling and sharing helps you remember what actually occurred and the tools that were used. When you remember the visions or words that the Lord showed you or told you, you can hold on to the truth that you received." – Bethel Sozo

As you can tell from this very short passage, none of it is biblical. When did Jesus tell Jairus' daughter, the woman with the issue of blood, Bartimaeus or the demoniac of Gadarene, all who experienced "Sozo," (*Healing*) that they needed to journal to hold unto the truth they received? The very moment the enemy gets the church off base, even slightly, he is in the door with a multifaceted plan.

The next step in the rebirth of so-called spirit writing came through what has been called "soaking." Anything designed to bring people closer to the Lord the enemy will twist so as to trap innocent victims. Here are some words from just one woman's story.

"I spent months immersing myself into the church teachings and music of the Jesus Culture at Bethel. (*Here is Bethel in Redding, California again*)

I started engaging in what is called, 'soaking.' Soaking is a practice of opening your mind and spirit to the 'lord' whilst listening to Christian" music. (*Notice the small case in 'lord.' This is a recurring pattern with people connected to Bethel*)

I gave up reading my Bible because I wanted new revelations from God, I had heard mentioned in so many sermons (including writings by Rick Joyner) that the Bible was being superseded by new revelations.

The people who only read the Bible were called 'Wordies' and these people ('The Wordies') were setting themselves up against the new spiritual move of 'god.' (*Notice the small case in "god."*)

The new spiritual movement was more important than the information in the Bible. So, I gave up my regular Bible reading and embraced soaking.

It's during this time that those who buy into new revelations from God, take out their Bibles and a pen."

She also told her readers that as she grew in this so-called spirit writing, at times, her body would shake and jerk. This is the same as what New Age participants report when they engage in intentional automatic writing. She said it was all part and parcel of the new thing in our day!

The statement she made, "I gave up reading my Bible because I wanted new revelations from God, I had heard mentioned in so many sermons (including writings by Rick Joyner) that the Bible was being superseded by new revelations," should cause us to be concerned. There are no new revelations from God.

Earlier we learned that the Bible tells us that the Canon of Scripture is closed.

"For I testify unto every man that heareth the words of the prophecy of this book, If any man shall add unto these things, God shall add unto him the plagues that are written in this book.

And if any man shall take away from the words of the book of this prophecy, God shall take away his part out of the book of life, and out of the holy city, and from the things which are written in this book." (Revelation 22:18-19)

This means that God is not giving new revelation to people today. He has spoken through His Word, and our job is to "contend for the faith that was once and for all entrusted to the saints." (Jude 1:3) We are not to seek anything that is not contained in the full counsel of God, the Bible. (Acts 20:27)

Here is a little more from this woman's story!

"The more I engrossed myself into Bethel church's teachings the more passionate I became about 'us' being 'right' and those that only followed the Bible being wrong. I could not see that this was happening. I no longer had any time for my family. I couldn't understand why my husband wasn't able to see the great "change" in me. I needed to be soaking and listening to my Jesus Culture music all the time. I was in a superior place with the Lord and I thought that Bible studies were a waste of time. I had the new anointing."

Be careful!

What was happening when this woman was listening to this music? What was she hearing through her headphones that she was unaware of?

"Take heed therefore that the light which is in thee be not darkness." (Luke 11:35)

Within days of reading her story, I encountered another. This man told me that when he is in need of an answer to a situation he has been taught to sit with his Bible. Turn on some soaking music, pick a verse of Scripture out of the hat and open himself up to the spirit realm. He would then begin to write whatever came into his head. His teachers told him that what came was Holy Ghost revelation from the Lord about the situation. Nowhere in any translation of the Bible can such a practice be found. The only place it can be found is in the teachings of the Spiritualist Church, through some so-called healing ministries, or on the New Age Oprah Winfrey Show. Why Oprah?

"Oprah Winfrey, who claims she is a Christian has been increasingly advocating New Age theology (*e.g., she says, 'I believe God is in all things'*) and denying that Jesus is the only way of salvation. She has said, 'One of the mistakes that human beings make is believing that there is only one way, when there are many paths to what you call God.' And elsewhere, 'I am a Christian, who believes that there are certainly many more paths to God other than Christianity.'" - Always Be Ready Apologetics Ministry

Winfrey, perhaps the most dangerous woman on the planet, is an advocate of automatic writing. Regarding Jimmy Page who wrote the song, "Stairway to heaven," said: "Page admits that it is one of the most popular songs ever in America and was given to him by the spirit world via automatic writing."

Some have taken the recording of that song and played it backwards at one twentieth of regular speed

66

and it revealed voices. The repetitious voices all the way through announce: "Here's to the path that I am on, the path of my sweet Satan." Another is: "I will sing because I live with Satan." This is what is called Backmasking.

Backmasking is a recording technique in which a sound or message is recorded backwards onto a track that is meant to be played forward. Backmasking is a deliberate process, whereas a message found through phonetic reversal may be unintentional or intended by Satan. It is not just in secular rock songs that such things are found, they are employed in some Christian worship. What is happening to people the world over when they are soaking, listening to some music?

Many Christian worship songs today contain messages subversive to the church. Subliminal messages in Christian worship are nothing new! Keith Green, a contemporary Christian music pianist, singer and songwriter, worshiper, and preacher, was one of the first to expose it. On July 28th, 1982, shortly after exposing these truths, he died suddenly and mysteriously in a small plane crash.

Since then, Wikipedia has carried the following article. "Backmasking was popularized by the Beatles, who used backward instrumentation on their 1966 album, 'Revolver.' Artists have since used Backmasking for artistic, comedic and satiric effect, on both analogue and digital recordings. The technique has also been used to censor words or phrases for 'clean' releases of explicit songs.

Backmasking has been a controversial topic in the United States since the 1980s, when allegations from Christian groups of its use for satanic purposes were made against prominent rock musicians, leading to record-burning protests and proposed anti-Backmasking legislation by state and federal governments."

Is it really taking place with worshipers today? Do any receive so-called worship songs through automatic or spirit writing? Where is it happening? Worship is singularly the most powerful quintessential of the church influencing the masses! Satan himself was a worshiper.

"The workmanship of your tambourines and of your flutes in you. In the day you were created, they were prepared.

You were the anointed cherub." (Ezekiel 28: 13b-14a LITV)

He knows what sort of worship is acceptable to the Lord and how to manipulate it into becoming worship of him. He also knows how to get such songs, into the hearts of God's worship teams. He excels at reaching the masses through subliminal messaging. He is not above using spirit or automatic writing in which the musician and songwriter believe they are receiving from the Lord Himself. Many wonderful worshipers may have already been duped.

MercyMe put out a song entitled, "I Can Only Imagine," and reputable sources claim that subliminally all the way through are words. Words that I am reluctant to write, but for the purpose of knowing the truth of what is happening they need recording.

"Imagine that I'm the only God. We've made sure we'll verve with the error of Satan." (*The word "verve" is archaic, meaning with "enthusiasm."*) It continues: "Wisdom of God the lonely one. Gnash-Damn thee, and only God. Damn the only God." (*The word "gnash" means to grind the teeth.*)

At first I completely dismissed this as total and complete, utter rubbish. Then, I felt led to listen to it both forwards and backwards. It was there! It was clearly heard on the recording I listened to!

How could this have come about? Something demonically supernatural had to have taken place during recording. Some of these groups unknowingly have been the victims of the enemy. Some have spent hours, days, weeks or even months waiting before the Lord. They longed for something special to lead God's people into His presence only to discover this. Still, it remains on the market today as is! One would think it would be changed especially since technology exists to remove it.

It is also heard in the Amy Grant recording of the same song. In Carmen's recording of "Destination is there," the words, "Satan worship the mark ... worship Satan," are clearly heard. The Resurrection Band's "Between heaven and hell" is Backmasked: "Yeah Lucifer promised me more, live for a week, ooh evil I take the mark."

We have seen that Backmasking has been intentionally created by others using technology. Hillsong in their recording of "Evermore," intentionally use what they call "Holy Backmasking." In any event, it's covert manipulation, no matter what the message's contents are! There are many such Backmasked songs in the churches today, these have been just a few.

Just as Jimmy Page wrote the secular song "Stairway to heaven" through automatic writing, there are also others who write worship songs through so-called spirit writing.

They get alone, turn on some soaking music and open themselves up to the spirit realm. What comes to their minds they write down! The question is, from what source in the spirit realm do these songs come? On the surface they sound great, just like when a Backmasked song is played forward. What is the result when these pieces are recorded?

In these last days, many have prophesied that the Lord is going to give to the church new songs. Songs so anointed that when people listen to them, salvation, healing and deliverance will flow like a river. They are correct! Such is the heart of The Father for the church today.

Of course, every time the Lord sets about to do something, the enemy is right there to hinder, destroy and lead people astray. When we listen to a worship song that has fallen foul to Backmasking, we hear nothing with the natural ear. However, auditory or visual, subliminal messages are stimuli that lay beneath our threshold of consciousness and are received in their entirety. This work of Satan upon the deeper levels of our being has been revived in our day.

His victims are the innocent! The young in Christ, those seeking for more of God, they are being raped by his evil hand. No one has given consent to the reception of these messages! Well did the LORD say in Genesis!

"And GOD saw that the wickedness of man was great in the earth, and that every imagination of the thoughts of his heart was only evil continually." (Genesis (6:5)

It's time to know all that is going on in the churches today. It's time not to get paranoid, but to have technical mechanisms put in place that will naturally protect our worship. It's time to root out and rip down, the high places that some of these so-called healing ministries have built into our denominations. It's time to protect "the Household of God" from the errors of what they call "something new!" It's time to open the church doors once more to abandonment, complete surrender of all. However, abandonment, "Expensive Grace" (grace uncompromised), that too has fallen foul of another gospel!

THE GRACE CARD

The sins of overemphasis and neglect have been around since time began. The pendulum of doctrine swings back and forth across the pages of time, caressing only that which is expedient to its expositors. In our day, the clock weight has swung once more, polluting true grace. It's not the first time, nor should Jesus tarry, will it be the last time. Every time error is found, the pendulum races in the opposite direction into over correction. The enemy loves this and laughs. Woefully, every time it swings back and forth many things become affected and not just in the church.

Let's take a short look at what the expositors of hyper-grace teach and line it up with the truth of the Word of God. Then, on we will go to see its consequences not only within the church, but in our nation. It is one more aspect of the unfolding plan of the enemy for the end.

"Hyper-grace" is a term used to describe a new wave of teaching that emphasizes the grace of God excluding other vital teachings such as repentance and confession of sin. Hyper-grace teachers maintain that "all sin, past, present, and future, has already been forgiven, so there is no need for a believer to ever confess it." – Joseph Prince, Destined to Reign

The hyper-grace teaching says that "when God looks at us He sees only a holy and righteous person." – John Bunjo

The conclusion of hyper-grace teaching is that their followers are not bound by Jesus' teaching, even as we are not under the Law; that believers are not responsible for their sin; and that anyone who disagrees is a Pharisaical legalist. In short, hyper-grace teachers pervert the grace of our God into a license for immorality (Jude 1:4) and flirt with Antinomianism. For these, the balance, "Jesus," on every tier of their lives is gone!

Jesus' words to the seven churches in the book of Revelation strongly contradict the idea that Christians never need to repent. To the church at Ephesus, Jesus said:

"Nevertheless I have somewhat against thee, because thou hast left thy first love." (Revelation 2:4)

Jesus rebukes five of the seven churches and demands repentance from them. (Revelation 2:4, 6, 20; 3:3, 15–19) Far from believers being unaccountable for their sin, they must answer to Jesus for their disobedience. (2 Corinthians 5:10)

Preachers of this hyper-grace doctrine discount the Old Testament and the Ten Commandments as irrelevant to New Testament believers. As expected, Bill Johnson of Bethel has been known to propagate this, but then again, he schools his millions of followers into thinking that Jesus had to be born again. He even attempts to prove this to the unwary by using the Bible.

Grace Revolution preachers, such as Joseph Prince, in their doctrinal statement: "The Bible is God's Word. It is inspired and accurate. It is our perfect guide in all matters of life." Still they teach that "Jesus' words spoken before His resurrection are part of the Old Covenant and no longer applicable to born-again believers." – S. Michael Houdmann, gotquestions.org

Is this true? If there is any uncertainty at all about the error then it's time to get our Bibles out and discover all we're being taught in church. The Bereans searched the word daily to see if what they learned was actually according to Scripture.

"These were more, noble than those in Thessalonica, in that they received the word with all readiness of mind, and searched the Scriptures daily, whether those things were so." (Acts 17:11)

In Mark 13:31, Jesus said, "Heaven and earth will pass away, but my words will never pass away." Before Jesus ascended into heaven, He promised that The Father would send the Holy Spirit who will teach you all things and will remind you of everything I have said to you. (John 14:26) If Jesus' words are no longer applicable to believers, why would we need reminding of them?

Hyper-grace teaching is a disastrous mixing of truth with error. An emphasis on the beauty and power of God's grace is good, but Prince and others neglect what Paul called the "whole counsel of God." (Acts 20:27) For example, it's true that Christians have been forgiven by God. However, that doesn't mean we never have to confess our sin. James 5:16 says, "Confess your sins to each other and pray for each other so that you may be healed."

If we are to confess our sins to each other, why would we not need to confess them to God, since every sin is ultimately a sin against God? (Psalm 51:4) Paul said, "I die daily," his death to sin was on a daily basis as he recognized the error in his heart, he confessed it. (1 Corinthians 15"31) Also, 1 John 1:9 gives clear instruction to believers about confessing sin. It begins with the word if.

"If we confess our sin, He is faithful and just to forgive our sin and to cleanse us from all unrighteousness."

This is a cause-and-effect statement implying that we cannot have the second without the first. As blood-bought children of God, we do not continue to confess our sin to be saved from hell. We confess and repent to maintain an intimate relationship with our Father. We are "positionally righteous" but "practically sinful."

To counter this argument, hyper-grace preachers deny that John's letters were written to believers. However, 1 John 2:1, begins with this:

"My little children, these things write I unto you, that ye sin not. And if any man sin, we have an advocate with the Father, Jesus Christ the righteous."

John was clearly writing to believers whom he personally knew. He indicated that his believing friends may indeed sin, and that when they did, they needed to confess it.

Hyper-grace expositors similarly claim that the Holy Spirit will never convict Christians of their sin and "The Moral Law" is no longer applicable. – Joseph Prince Destined to Reign

Mature Christians should recognize this fallacy right away. Every disciple of Christ has felt the overwhelming conviction of the Holy Spirit when he or she has sinned. Jesus calls the Holy Spirit "the Spirit of Truth." (John 15:26) Truth, by its very definition, will not tolerate anything false. This then brings about some questions.

Why is it, we who live and move and have our being in "Truth" tolerate this kind of error in our churches? Why is it we are so insensitive to the Holy

Spirit that we cannot feel the Spirit's check, especially when so many place so much emphasis upon the senses? Why is the enemy in such a panic in our day and time? Perhaps the answer to these questions is we are reading the Bible instead of studying it! Maybe we have abandoned the written Word for other things! Satan knows that his end is at hand and he is out to deceive as many as possible as he brings together his end time's strategy!

When the Spirit of Truth abides in a believing heart, (1 Corinthians 6:19) He brings conviction about anything that is not truth, leading us into a right relationship. (John 16:13)

In summary, some of what the hyper-grace preachers teach is valid. We are certainly saved by grace, not by works. (Ephesians 2:8–9) God's grace is marvelous, great, and free. (1 Timothy 1:14) However, hyper-grace teaching is out of proportion to the rest of Scripture. Any time one doctrine is emphasized to the exclusion of the rest, we fall into error because we fail to "correctly handle" the Word. (2 Timothy 2:15) Scripture tells us to rightly divide the Word of Truth. (2 Timothy 2:15)

Jesus is full of both "grace and truth." (John 1:14) The two are in delicate balance, and a tip to either side can result in a false gospel. We must always compare any new teaching with the "whole counsel of God" and learn to disregard anything that veers even slightly from the truth. (1 John 4:1)

When the church is taken captive by error, this in turn overspreads our communities through our work, schools and eventually into the halls of big business and government by those who carry their belief structure with them. Economies soar and crumble, bringing about military conflict. Lives are lost in their thousands and millions as the heroes of the faith at their own peril stand up against the wiles of the devil. Miserably, their suffering comes about at the hands of church going people. Let's go back in time to another day when hyper-grace filled the pulpits of the past and learn from its consequences.

The capitulation of the German church to Hitler came in 1933 when he ascended to power. Many were left astounded, wondering how the "church of Luther" came to such a watered down place. The answer is that the true gospel of "Expensive Grace" had been lost. On the one hand, the church had become marked by formalism. That meant, going to church and hearing that God just loves and forgives everyone, so it doesn't really matter how you live. On the other hand, there was legalism, or salvation by law and good works. Legalism meant that God loves you because you have pulled yourself together and are trying to live a good, disciplined life.

Nazi Germany in World War Two was responsible for the death of millions. "The Holocaust!" History says that these things happened as a result of the evil that arose in the heart of a nation suffering from the wounds that resulted from their humiliation and defeat in World War One. While there was an element of truth to that historical fact, we cannot forget the reason for why such a wound went unhealed. Why was such evil able to rise with rapid speed and destruction? These atrocities were the indirect result of a church that had become lukewarm and ready to be spewed out of the Lord's mouth. (Revelation 3:16) It came about because people were taught that no matter what they did, it was all covered under grace.

Dietrich Bonhoeffer, the great German pastor and theologian, was asked in 1943 how it was possible for the church to sit back and let Hitler and the Nazis seize absolute power. Bonhoeffer's reply: "It was the teaching of cheap grace." He described cheap or hyper-grace as:

"The preaching of forgiveness without requiring repentance. Cheap grace is grace without discipleship, grace without the cross, and grace without Jesus Christ, living and incarnate." - The Cost of Discipleship 1937

In essence, he was saying that they were taught: "Of course you have sinned, still everything is forgiven, so you can stay as you are and enjoy the consolations of forgiveness." The main defect of such a proclamation is that it contains no demand for discipleship, no accountability. In contrast to this is expensive grace.

"Expensive Grace" confronts us as a gracious call to follow Jesus; it comes as a word of forgiveness to the broken spirit and the contrite heart. (Psalm 51:17) It requires absolute abandonment to Jesus. It's expensive because it compels us to submit to the yoke of Christ and follow Him; it's grace because Jesus says: "My yoke is easy and my burden is light." (Matthew 11:30)

Hyper-grace allows the church to become "secularized," accommodating the demands of obedience to Jesus to the requirements of society. In this way, the world becomes culturally Christianized, and grace becomes its common property. The hazard of this is that the gospel is cheapened, and obedience to the living Christ is gradually lost beneath formalism and ritual, so that in the end, grace is literally sold for monetary gain.

Bonhoeffer took a gallant stand and from a Nazi jail cell he wrote because few listened when he spoke. To the church he was the one in error. To the Nazis, he was dangerous. In the end this hero of the faith was hanged by the neck until dead.

In our day, voices must again rise regardless of consequence to help love the church back from the brink. Hyper-grace in our day should send out grave warning signals in our beloved Canada.

In the 1960s, Northern Ireland was on the verge of war. The recognized church had fallen victim to hyper-grace. Going to church on Sunday was something that did not originate in a heart of love. It was the established thing to do. No mention of sin or its consequences was preached in the sermons. It was a social gospel! People taught justification of sin without the justification of the sinner. Grace alone does everything they said, and so everything could stay as it was before. No opportunities were ever given for people to come clean with the truth. So these cultural Christians lived like the rest of the world and followed a life of sectarianism.

In 1969 there commenced another bloody chapter in Ulster's endless civil war. As bodies began to pile up on the sidewalks, people in the churches turned a blind eye. It was just the same as in Hitler's Nazi Germany. Ministers, although knowing who the terrorists were, sitting in their churches, turned a blind eye.

Roman Catholic priests offered absolution to I.R.A. gunmen moments after they murdered innocent women and children. Hyper-grace had taught them their atrocities were all covered by grace. Conviction of sin was far from their hearts. Thousands died, and still today, the perpetrators continue believing they are going to heaven, heroes of a cause. A great surprise awaits their passing!

What about today, here in North America? What about the churches we attend? We too have progressed down the road of "hyper-grace" for many years. Many of the issues of our time, the breakdown of the family, divorce, sexual promiscuity, and abortion, just to name a few, have become nothing more than a series of lifestyle decisions. All around us, there are those who say, well, these are not really wrong, they are just choices. If it's wrong, don't worry, there's grace. A great example of this misapplication of grace is found in the rise of the homosexual movement, specifically the delusion often called "gay marriage."

Many practicing homosexuals and lesbians are ordained to the pulpit annually! This is hyper-grace gone off the rails. The government bowed the knee to such perversion and legalized same-sex marriage! This caused many truth believing churches to scramble to change their constitution! Their goal: to guard against further laws requiring them to perform same-sex unions.

The only lawful union recognized by the Bible is the union between one man and one woman. (Genesis 2:24, Proverbs 18:22, Matthew 19: 3-6) True believers are called homophobic for standing up and speaking the truth of the Word of God. We are challenged to become more inclusively accepting.

"What fellowship hath righteousness with unrighteousness? And what communion hath light with darkness?" (2 Corinthians 6:14)

Hyper-grace in Canadian churches opened the door for so-called Christian lawmakers to turn a blind eye to other legislation. In Canada, all forms of polygamy, and some informal multiple sexual relationships, are illegal under Section 293 of the Criminal Code of Canada. However, for a long time, the law banning polygamy has not been efficient. This is an example of a lukewarm church producing apathy within law enforcement.

Canada is a nation built upon the principle of the sovereignty of God as outlined in "The Charter of Rights and Freedoms," "The Constitution Act" before that and "The British North America Act" at first. However, because of secularization brought on by hyper-grace in the church, she stands on the verge of disaster.

In many parts of the country, Muslim Sharia Law is gaining momentum at the municipal level. In fact, the provincial governments of Canada for years have tacitly recognized Sharia law for Canada's Muslim minority by sending multiple welfare checks to polygamous Muslim men who raise multiple families. Of course the recipients have found and use loopholes in the law to their benefit. This in turn has attracted other Muslims to Canada's shores. Many of those who have come are Jihadists.

The Canadian government has banned more than 50 terrorist organizations. Who will ever forget the day when a radicalized masked gunman killed Cpl. Nathan Cirillo as he stood guard at the National War Memorial in Ottawa? With that, the march towards the precipice of gloom for Canada surged forward.

That week a 13-year-old, Jackson Reid, of the Seaforth Highlanders of Canada Army Cadet Corps, completed Nathan's guard at the memorial. A young lad stood up!

As the church falls into disarray, where are the adults who will stand on guard for the truth of the Word of God? Sorrowfully, we would be hard pressed to find them. They sit, bound by apathy, in their social clubs, which was once the church.

In just about every community there are both multi-faith and interfaith gatherings. In interfaith, darkness and light come together. While a cultural Christian may bring a watered down message, Hindus, Islamists or the followers of Baha'i offer worship their way under the symbols of their beliefs intermingled. To who is this worship offered? Certainly not to the Lord!

Naturally, they justify their actions by saying they are being culturally inclusive. All the while, the real church is silent! Afraid to stand up and be counted! It's the hyper-grace message of a passive church that is largely responsible for creating the environment that permits these things to thrive.

This is the problem with multiculturalism, it's a plague in the heart of Canada. It permits those who come here to fly the flags from their former countries over their homes. The only flag that should be flown is the Maple Leaf. What we need is a melting pot, bringing all under a Canadian identity. Then again, we need to have our Canadian character restored to the truth of the gospel. Without this, it will continue unabated as Canada plunges deeper into the darkness of death. If we don't stand up against this hyper-grace message now the blood of our children, as with Nathan Cirillo, will again run in the streets of our cities.

When I refer to our true Canadian Christian identity, I am in no way making reference to the error of the Christian Identity Movement. The Christian Identity Movement is a name that applies to a variety of religious cults all identified by racist, anti-Semitic principles.

These cults are typically found among radical anti-government, extremist, right-wing and "survival groups." Christian Identity cults are connected by various unbiblical theological similarities, mostly centered on a white supremacist mindset that seeks to replace national Israel with American whites being the chosen people of God. Anglo-Israelism is still alive and well on planet earth. This racist theology is followed by thousands in Canada and over 50,000 people in the United States. The largest Christian Identity Movement group is the infamous Ku Klux Klan.

When morality by the hand of a lukewarm church becomes so subjective that it has lost all meaning, the right to freedom of speech, religion, assembly, and the press is stripped away or redefined.

In Nazi Germany, when they came for the mentally challenged, the people felt that this was not their problem. Their right to life and liberty meant nothing. When they took away the gypsies to the death camps that was not the concern of the masses. Their right to equality, fraternity, an ethical relationship between people, found no place in society. When they tried to exterminate the Jews, the German people chose to turn a blind eye. The perpetrators of these atrocities justified their actions. The people believed they were still going to heaven! They believed in hyper-grace. If a stop is not put to this message in our churches today, history will repeat itself.

Someone once said that if an aircraft leaves Toronto with a destination marked for Halifax, Nova Scotia, and the flight course is off by just a few degrees upon departure, if not corrected at the outset, it could wind up somewhere in the Atlantic off the coast of

Maine, USA. This is the effect that the winds of doctrine produce. It's not the 95 percent truth that will take the body of Christ of course, it's the five percent error that will potentially run us into the ditch. Benjamin Franklin, even though an unbeliever, wrote a poem and penned it better than I ever could.

> "For the want of a nail the shoe was lost,
> For the want of a shoe the horse was lost,
> For the want of a horse the rider was lost,
> For the want of a rider the battle was lost,
> For the want of a battle the kingdom was lost,
> And all for the want of a horseshoe-nail."

How do we stop it? It's going to take more than voting in the elections, as vital as that is, to change the course we are on. What we need is a personal revival that will shake the very foundations of our being! One that will pull us out of our coma of complacency! A national revival that will return us to holding a powerful influence over the destiny of Canada may not come because of our proximity to the end! Only dedicated people can see this awesome country restored to the vision our forefathers had.

We need to run quickly from the messengers of hyper-grace! Remove them from the pulpit if they refuse to repent! Yes, and if need be, we need not a reformation, rather we need a non-violent revolution within the church. A revolution in which every perversion of grace and faith are swept from the church forever. One that brings to a dead stop all so-called manifestations and see restored the full manifestation as seen in the Word of God. An uprising that will carry us back to the truth of the "whole counsel of God." (Acts 20:27)

Are we ready to do our part for Jesus? The enemy's plans are advancing while we sleep. Are we willing to stand on guard for Canada? Then let's take a stand today, right where we are!

EVIL IN THE PRAYER CLOSET

The road towards the end has been paved and soon the lawless one will appear!

"Even him, whose coming is after the working of Satan with all power and signs and lying wonders." (2 Thessalonians 2:9)

The lie is happening all around us! The beast of Revelation, the world system and the false prophet, its leader, are assembling in the earth today. How do we know this?

Just one quick look at world politics and economics shows clearly that they are among us. A glance within many churches should convince us that the lying signs and wonders are already in operation. These lying signs and wonders, the Lord told us would be with us through the end times. (Matthew 24:24)

If we thought that these signs and wonders would take place outside the church, think again! Jesus said they have purpose and "if possible shall deceive the very elect." Where are the believers found? It's us they are designed to deceive. In the earlier chapters, we found them in the church!

Through every page, we learned that Satan's attack has been on every tier of truth in the church. Lies abound when it comes to understanding the Master's presence. The glory cloud they relegate to a few specs of glitter, orbs of light, angel feathers or a thousand other things. People in dire need of salvation and healing are cheated out of the instantaneous to suffer week after week of sessions. Even for those seeking the face of God, Satan has twisted it into spirit writing as people open themselves to the spirit realm. These precious people have no idea who or what is answering their cries to what they believe is the Holy Spirit. We have seen how the enemy continues to violate the hearts of people in worship.

There is a common denominator, a single earthly source, where these falsehoods originate. Although the Bethel church in Redding, California is the catalyst within Christian circles, they are not the incendiary in the world. Who they are, we will discover later. In the meantime the enemy continues to infiltrate other sacred areas of life.

All around us people in prayer have called for revival! What they have in some places they call renewal! Renewal is a far cry from real revival! In fact, the word renewal, as they apply it to these meetings, occurs nowhere in the Bible. The word renew does appear, but nothing in the context they attribute to it today. Lamentations 5:21, says:

"Turn thou us unto thee, O LORD, and we shall be turned; renew our days as of old." Hebrews 6:6 speaks about being restored to Jesus after tasting the Word of God and then walking away. Psalm 51:10, calls upon the Lord to: "Create in me a clean heart, O God; and renew a right spirit within me."

On the other hand, the word "revive" certainly does appear in Scripture. (Psalm 85:6, Habakkuk 3:2)

During the history of the world, there have been seven historic revivals that resulted in total and complete transformations. Whole cities were transformed! Crime rates fell dramatically! Schools, workplaces, big business and governments all felt the effects of change. Incidentally, seven is the number of completion.

Along with those revivals came many counterfeits, similar to much of what today are the earmarks of renewal. Let's turn to some of the greats of historic revival to prove a point.

"At the first, revival was true and pure, but after a few weeks we had to watch for counterfeits." - John Wesley

"The dawn of revival is a major opportunity ... for deception to find a foothold through counterfeits and copies which - though seemingly harmless will destroy the soul." - Jessie Penn-Lewis

"A religion of mere emotion and sensationalism is the most terrible of curses that can come upon a people. The absence of reality is sad enough, but when aggravated by pretense of godliness, this is a deadly sin." - Samuel Chadwick

Have you ever stood at the back of a meeting and stayed out of the flow, kept your head clear and watched carefully all that transpired? I don't mean being judgmental, but seeking the heart of God for all that you see happening? Try it once and it will stir in your heart a question! What on earth is a counterfeit? Discernibly, a counterfeit is a copy of something real, but have you ever wondered whether the phenomenon you were observing was real or false?

Such a journey should lead us back to the Bible in search of some benchmarks! Since our doctrinal statements claim that the Bible is our final authority on everything, then all we are seeing must line up with its truths.

The first thing we will discover is that much of it is lukewarm at best. Some of it is shallow! People are seeking the external when Jesus begins with the internal, and they claim it's all by the hand of the Eternal.

"I have rejected him; for God sees not as man looks; for man looks at the outward appearance, but God looks at the heart." (1 Samuel 16:7, Benton)

As soon as we understand this principle, just like John Wesley, Jessie Penn-Lewis and Samuel Chadwick, we get launched on a search for the signposts to lying signs and wonders.

"Even him, whose coming is after the working of Satan with all power and signs and lying wonders,

And with all deceivableness of unrighteousness in them that perish; because they received not the love of the truth, that they might be saved.

And for this cause God shall send them strong delusion, that they should believe a lie." (2 Thessalonians 2:2-11)

The work of Satan is displayed in all kinds of counterfeit miracles, signs and wonders, and in every sort of evil that deceives. His goal is to prevent people in our churches from getting saved. We all know that the church is filled with nominal Christians at best. More are cultural Christians than actual believers. So why is God sending a strong delusion? (Verse 11)

The Bible makes it clear why this delusion comes in the end times. They perish because they blatantly turned their backs on the truth. They tasted the good word of God, and the powers of the world to come, still they turned to follow the way of Balaam. It's for this reason God sends them a powerful delusion, so that by their own choice, they believe the lie. There is a very grave warning in these verses.

"For it is impossible for those who were once enlightened, and have tasted of the heavenly gift, and were made partakers of the Holy Ghost!

And have tasted the good word of God, and the powers of the world to come,

If they shall fall away, to renew them again unto repentance; seeing they crucify to themselves the Son of God afresh, and put him to an open shame." (Hebrews 6: 4-6)

These are condemned because they refuse the truth and delight in wickedness. Simply put, God sends a strong delusion to those who choose not to believe the full gospel of Christ. How long will someone have, after turning to error? That will depend on the person. Will all who are innocently trapped by error be condemned? NO! This Scripture is implying that those who continue to advance in error can eventually arrive at that place. They can, and some will, come to the place of complete apostasy. They will be given time to repent. They will resist the leading of the Holy Spirit, choosing instead the counterfeit, until it is eventually too late. Instead, they will choose the external, (*cloud of glitter, so-called gold dust, and oil on hands, angel feathers, orbs of light, spirit writing, the psychology of Sozo sessions, hyper-grace or even more*) and reject the internal instant transformation. These are those who will have settled for less than real revival.

Its man's choice whether or not to accept and believe the truth of Jesus Christ as presented in the Scriptures. To receive the love that God offers in keeping with His teachings is ours to make. "For this is the love of God, that we keep his commandments." (1 John 5:3a)

Conversely, to know the truth and not obey it is to face the wrath of God.

"The wrath of God is being revealed from heaven against all the godlessness and wickedness of men who suppress the truth by their wickedness." (Romans 1:18)

Frankly speaking, there is no more dangerous condition for man than to know the truth and compromise it. To do so is to harden the heart and make God's condemnation sure. Watch out when God himself is out to deceive a person – who's going to stop Him?

Remember again that Peter warned against the way of Balaam, the false teacher; Jude against the error of Balaam, the preacher who sells his gifting; and John against the doctrine of Balaam, compromise. (2 Peter 2:15, Jude 11, Revelation 2:14)

Matthew reminds us: "For false Christs and false prophets will appear and perform great signs and miracles to deceive even the elect, if that were possible." (Matthew 24:24 *Paraphrased*)

The false revelatory individual will perform great signs and wonders, some with the unintentional aim of deceiving the elect. Some command the attention of great crowds. Once more, those in the churches are the targets! As great and marvelous as the wonders may seem, as awe-inspiring and as slick as their presentations, how can we tell if God is behind them or not? It's time, once more, to test the spirits to see if they actually line up with God's Word.

"Hereby know ye the Spirit of God: Every spirit that confesseth that Jesus Christ is come in the flesh is of God." (1 John 4:2)

Every spirit that directs us to Jesus, and not the manifestation, is of God. He we should follow.

In our day, people go to meetings only for the manifestation and not to experience Jesus on the inside. Every spirit that points us to the full counsel of the Word of God is of The Father. Simply put, a false prophet will lead us to worship another Jesus, a Jesus other than the one in our final authority, the Bible. They will teach us another way to connect with God! Earlier we saw how some accomplish that.

Jesus warned us of our day saying, "And then shall many be offended, and shall betray one another, and shall hate one another.

And many false prophets shall rise, and shall deceive many.

And because iniquity shall abound, the love of many shall wax cold." (Matthew 24:10-12)

Again, the Lord warned that many will be deceived! In our time, many have already turned away from the faith. Churches grow emptier by the week. Many have long forgotten the great commission, to win the lost. People invite others to church, not to meet with Jesus, but because some manifestation is taking place in their church or some new teaching is flying around.

The environment today is one of people turning away from the true gospel and going after a copy, a counterfeit. The false prophets take advantage of such times and come to deceive, take advantage of wickedness and promote selfishness. As love grows cold, they exhort the backslider to pursue wickedness, or put another way, to follow anything but holiness! Of course they don't say, "Come with me and pursue wickedness." It's all covered in a cloak of clouded light. Only they are right and everyone else wrong. Anyone who brings them the truth in love they excommunicate from their midst. They forget these words:

"Woe unto them that call evil good, and good evil; that put darkness for light, and light for darkness; that put bitter for sweet, and sweet for bitter!" (Isaiah 5:20)

The way, the error and the doctrine of Balaam have come upon us like a tsunami wave! Be warned!

"Beware of false prophets, which come to you in sheep's clothing, but inwardly they are ravening wolves." (Matthew 7:15)

How will we know them? The very next verse holds the answer for us!

"Ye shall know them by their fruits. Do men gather grapes of thorns, or figs of thistles?" (Verse 16)

Âh, the much quoted verse about fruit! No, not manifestations, instead fruit. Of course, many say: "fruit inspectors, we don't need them." These quote the Scripture, "judge not that ye be not judged." (Matthew 7:1)

What we don't need are fruit inspectors that look through the eyes of obsession. However, we do need inspectors who: "judge not according to the appearance, but judge righteous judgment." (John 7:24) In these last days, we need to see the fruit of lives in ministry.

What is the deposit of God an itinerant minister leaves behind them? Is it one of souls saved, lives transformed, cities changed and crime rates lowered? Are they known for this or for the so-called manifestations, a new message or new anointing? A great litmus test for the itinerant prophet or visiting minister is what people say about them.

A telltale sign of a false prophet, one thing that will give them away, is if men speak highly of them – if people speak well of them all the time.

"Woe to you when all men speak well of you, for that is how their fathers treated the false prophets." (Luke 6:26).

In contrast, Israel and the leaders of the day persecuted God's true prophets, they weren't well accepted. Paul says they were "stoned, sawn in two, put to death, destitute, persecuted and mistreated." (Hebrews 11:37)

That is the treatment true ministers of truth get from the "crowd." So it was with John the Baptist – he was beheaded. Persecution is the treatment Jesus received and it is no different for a real prophet or apostle today either. It goes without saying that a false prophet when confronted with the truth will claim they are being persecuted for the gospel. Interestingly, not many, if any are killed for their message. How popular is their message?

Dietrich Bonhoeffer's message of true grace opposing cheap or hyper-grace got him hanged by the neck until dead. Corrie ten Boom's messages of love found her in a lice infested Nazi prison camp. Because of her faith, Nora Lamb was placed in front of a firing squad. On the command to fire, the guns exploded and she fell to the ground unharmed. The Lord graciously spared her. Many others have paid the ultimate price.

All around the globe, the Lord is raising up preachers expounding one last "Final Warning." Naturally, they are unpopular! In fact, many with extreme intensity of emotion or conviction come against them while they defend their own leaders, when challenged by the final authority, the Word of God.

Many itinerant preachers hold that their theologies are the result of the Lord restoring things long forgotten by the church. Every time the Lord restores something in the church, that restoration must stay compliant with the standards of His Word. In recent years there has been what many call the restoration of the five-fold ministry. Nothing wrong with that as long as those in office walk in line with and meet the criteria of the Word of God.

Newton said: "For every action there is an equal and opposite reaction." Applied to the church in our day it means that for every real Apostle that rises, there is a false apostle. How do we identify a real Apostle?

"Am I not an apostle? Am I not free? Have I not seen Jesus Christ our Lord? Are not ye my work in the Lord?" (1 Corinthians 9:1)

Paul was met by the resurrected Christ on the Damascus Road. This happened after the ascension. What he is speaking about was his qualifications as an Apostle. Therefore, only those who have had an actual encounter with the resurrected Christ can hold such office. There are many today who embrace the idea that an Apostle is someone who sits as the under-shepherd of a multiple of churches. As with every error, it's not the majority of correctness, it's the small percentage of error that leads us away from the Word and lands us in trouble. After appointment as an Apostle, in the Word, they gave great witness of the Master's resurrection.

"And with great power gave the apostles witness of the resurrection of the Lord Jesus: and great grace was upon them all." (Acts 4:33)

Everywhere they went they persuaded, convinced people, of the reality of the resurrection. What did the apostles we have met persuade or convince us of at the last meeting? As soon as they open their mouths, what is in their hearts becomes known.

Before we move on, let's take a look at the new wave that is engulfing the church. It's time to discover how the enemy has invaded the intimacy of our prayers.

Prophetic Prayer! Intercession – that too has been hijacked by the enemy camp. Prophetic Prayer or Prophetic Intercession, founded by Mike Bickle, a self-styled apostle, quickly became an unbiblical practice that seeks to ascribe to prayers power and privilege that have no foundation in Scripture.

A statement made by the founder begins to open our eyes even more about how error in the church takes hold.

"We're not absent for the great tribulation, now listen carefully, the church causes the great tribulation. What I mean by that – it's the church, it's the praying church under Jesus' leadership that's losing the judgment in the great tribulation in the way that Moses stretched forth his rod and prayed and loosed the judgments upon Pharaoh. The church in the tribulation is in the position that Moses was before Pharaoh, but it won't be a Pharaoh and Egypt, it'll be the great end time Pharaoh called the Antichrist and the book of Revelation is a book about the judgments of God on the Antichrist loosed by the praying church."

Tremendous as his words may seem, at their heart lie several theologies that err according to Scripture. The first questionable statement is: "We're not absent for the great tribulation." Obviously he holds to a post-tribulation rapture idea whereas most believe the church will be taken out beforehand. We believe this because during the tribulation God's wrath is poured out. The Word of the Lord offers us a sure and steadfast promise.

"For God hath not appointed us to wrath, but to obtain salvation by our Lord Jesus Christ." (1 Thessalonians 5:9)

Bickle, further states that the church through prayer will bring in the tribulation and this will take place when the church prays for it to happen. We know the end will be brought about by the error of the church, but it will not happen one minute before God's timing. Perhaps this is one such error! These people believe they can bring it about. He says that: "The book of Revelation is a book about the judgments of God on the Antichrist loosed by the praying church." Only a mind clouded by darkness could make such a statement.

The book of Revelation is loaded with wonderful things. The marriage supper of the Lamb. (Revelation 16:6-9) That day when every tear is wiped away. (Revelation 21:4) Spending eternity with Him in glory. The glory that the book of Revelation describes includes the sounds, colors and precious stones listed. (Revelation 4:3, 18:22) Every single one carries wonderful symbolism. Can you imagine the joy the Lord will feel as He takes us for a walk by heaven's river? (Revelation 22:1) Just you and Him together in the oneness He prayed about in John 17. How can anyone miss all that and only see judgments?

The practitioners of prophetic prayer believe they bring new revelation. Remember, the Bible tells us that the canon of Scripture is closed. There are no new revelations to so-called prophets today. He has spoken through His Word and our job is to "vie for the faith that was once and for all entrusted to the saints." (Jude 1:3) We are not to seek anything that is not contained in the full counsel of God, the Bible. What Bickle has said is nowhere mentioned in Scripture. Let me make that abundantly clear.

A real prophet, and they are among us, will speak only what is contained in the Cannon. (Joel 2:28, Acts 2:17) All proclamations made by them, line up with God's calendar in accordance with His timing. If someone tells us anything as a prophetic utterance and we cannot find it in the Word, it's not the Lord speaking.

Prophetic prayer is usually described as the act of commanding God's "prophetic vision" to be fulfilled on the earth, with the result that God's will is accomplished. Prophetic prayer is taught in some charismatic ministries as a means of bringing God's judgment on the earth and ushering in God's Kingdom. In this, they claim that their prayers alter the course of future events.

Prophetic prayer is aimed at individuals, so they will fulfill their "prophetic purpose," (*their service in God's plan*), and their purpose in the world in general, so God's desires are accomplished on earth. Jesus, however, in teaching us to pray in Matthew 6, shows us to submit to God's will; it does not teach that we possess special powers to actualize God's will. This evil spirit loosed in the earth would seek to bring a premature end of all things. There are many out there today who would like things to wrap up sooner than expected. However, God's plan will come to pass on His exact timetable that He has not shared with us. (Matthew 24:36; 25:13; Mark 13:32; Luke 12:37-47) He has told us what He is waiting for. He is waiting for the precious fruit of the earth.

98

(James 5:7) He is waiting for us to reach as many as possible. Bickle on the other hand would seek to end it prematurely.

Demanding His judgment to fall and His kingdom to come at the will of the "prophet" is arrogant and possibly blasphemous. The Lord is the one who will bring to pass all His will: "What I have said, that will I bring about; what I have planned, that will I do." (Isaiah 46:11)

When someone engages in prophetic prayer, he is not asking for God's will to be done; he is commanding God's will to be done, and he believes that as:

"Moses stretched forth his rod and prayed and loosed the judgments upon Pharaoh. The church in the tribulation is in the position that Moses was before Pharaoh, but it won't be a Pharaoh and Egypt, it'll be the great end time Pharaoh called the Antichrist." – Mike Bickle

This is a perfect example where the Word is taken way out of context. Yes, Moses did command judgment to fall, and it did; however, it did so at the command of God and in the timing of God. In this, it was initiated by God and not man.

These teachings came about when people preached about calling things into existence. For this premise they used Romans 4:17. The latter part of that verse says: "God, who quickeneth the dead, and calleth those things which be not as though they were." Beyond a doubt, the Lord can use us in this way. However, some think that we can, just like the Lord, create and speak things into existence in our time. What they miss is the aspect of God's will and His timing. Without both of those, we can speak all day long and nothing will happen.

It was here that the enemy ran this off the rails. It's through prophetic prayer the enemy has invaded the prayer closet.

They are quoted as saying in their defense: "Well, we would expect you to be against it since you haven't had the experience." That is Gnosticism! (*Esoteric knowledge*) It's believing that they are elevated to a higher level of comprehension which the uninitiated have no understanding of. All false teachers, prophets or apostles resort to this argument. The very moment they use it, the true nature of their hearts they expose!

Those who teach prophetic prayer point to Jesus' model prayer, which includes the words, "your kingdom come, your will be done on earth as it is in heaven." (Matthew 6:10 ISV) This verse, they say, teaches that we should demand God's will on the world around us. As a modern-day prophet speaks God's words "on the earth" or "into the atmosphere," he believes that he changes his environment to conform to God's command and paves the way for God's purpose. They have it backwards. God's purpose paves the way for a man to speak.

Those who practice prophetic prayer believe they do not just predict what will happen; they believe they actually create the thing predicted! "The Tribulation." Prophetic prayer, they believe, actually brings into existence its own answer. The Bible clearly declares that God alone decides when, where, and how He will act. We are to pray for Him to act according to His perfect will and timing, not according to our own.

These people use watered down versions of the Bible to formulate their position such as the International Standard Version. We need to be careful what we take from such translations of the Bible. You will

100

notice the words of this translation. "Your kingdom come, your will be done 'ON' earth as it is in heaven." (Matthew 6:10 NIV) Many weak versions use the word "ON" in their translations. As a result, man develops deceptive theologies. Nowhere in the original texts is the word "ON" used. The King James Version says: "Thy kingdom come. Thy will be done, 'IN' earth, as it is in heaven." The use of the word "IN" changes the context of the verse. "In earth" implies His will is to be done "IN" us, not in the atmosphere. We are the earth spoken of in the Master's Prayer. "We have this treasure in earthen vessels." (2 Corinthians 4:7) We were created from the dust of the earth. (Genesis 2:7) Nothing in the Lord's Prayer tells us anything about changing our environment or the future!

As a point of note, the New International Version deletes 64,000 words from the official translations.

Those who teach prophetic prayer also believe that God uses prophets to provide answers to other people's prayers. If someone is seeking an answer to prayer, God may urge a prophet to speak prophetically so that the other person's prayer will be answered. The Bible, however, teaches that the answer to our prayers is not dependent on any "prophet" in this world. Today, many faced with certain situations flock to these so-called prophets for a word in their situation. This nonsense places the so-called prophet as being a mediator.

"For there is one God, and one mediator between God and men, the man Christ Jesus." (1 Timothy 2:5)

Is prophetic prayer biblical? In these areas, NO! Still, it does not hold a candle to even greater errors released during our day!

All this comes from the false apostles, prophets and teachers among us. They secretly introduce destructive heresies, even denying the sovereign Lord. Many will follow their shameful ways and will bring the way of truth into disrepute. If the enemy can bring heresy into the prayer closet, what will be safe from him?

THE HORN MANIFESTO

Here are some definitive benchmarks to test a false prophet or teacher.

"But there were false prophets also among the people, even as there shall be false teachers among you, who privily shall bring in damnable heresies, even denying the Lord that bought them, and bring upon themselves swift destruction.

And many shall follow their pernicious ways; by reason of whom the way of truth shall be evil spoken of.

And through covetousness shall they with feigned words make merchandise of you: whose judgment now of a long time lingereth not, and their damnation slumbered not." (2 Peter 2: 1-3)

They deny the sovereignty of God! How many preachers have we heard say that recently? Not many I bet! Peter tells us they secretly introduce heresy, a little here and a little there, bending the truth, perverting leadership one by one. Like Balaam, they are greedy for material gain. They exploit the congregation with words the congregants, want to hear. Rest assured, says verse three, their damnation does not slumber.

There are many who deliver titillating sermons! Those who pander to the needs and desires of the audience. They promise blessings, prosperity and healing. Everything the average Canadian wants more of and none of what they don't. There is no mention of sin, repentance, confession, or obedience in any individually given word. Just one blessing after another announced to the world. At the very least, you would think that when sin is detected, the person would be taken aside privately and told. It does not happen. All people want today, is some positive word of blessing from the Lord. Why?

"For the time is coming when people will not put up with sound doctrine, but having itching ears, they will accumulate for themselves teachers to suit their own desires, and will turn away from listening to the truth and wander away to myths." (2 Timothy 4:3-4) That time is here!

False teachers are those who teach according to what the people want to hear. Oh, what a temptation there is for the paid pastor, who, knowing he must preach the full Word of God, also knows that the tithes and offerings will diminish as a result.

The very fact that many counterfeits are present in some churches is a confirmation that the real thing is available. Be warned the enemy is seeking to divert us from the straight and narrow to the rapidly increasing queue at the off-ramps.

The end is at hand and all that the Lord promised for our day is coming to pass ever-increasingly. Proportional to the speed that things are unfolding before our eyes, the enemy's end time's manifesto is in like manner making the headlines. Some of it is hidden in a world of the ridiculous. On the surface we might say, how can people believe that? People believe it in their millions all around us. They believe it since one error after another was introduced to the church that acceptance became natural for most. Many true Bible believing followers pay little attention to it because of how silly it really sounds. The enemy is counting on that!

One such false teacher, an instructor of Satan's ridiculous, is Tom Horn. People in their millions flock to conferences and their television sets to hear him. Timothy says:

"They are always making trouble, because they are people whose thinking has been confused. They have lost their understanding of the truth. They think that devotion to God is a way to get rich." (1 Timothy 6:5 ERV)

These are they who once had possession of the truth and lost it by their own fault. They fell away from the truth, and are now twice dead. For some of them, the Bible was not enough, so they turned to the realm of science fiction to explain Eschatology! One such expositors of this kind of shame is Tom Horn. Here again we see the drawing away from the Word of God as the enemy's plan marches on.

To come to his conclusions, Horn uses books not included in the Cannon of Scripture. He makes assumptions based on the Apocryphal books contained in most Roman Catholic Bibles. Such books as Enoch, Baruch, Tobit, Jasher, Judith, and additions to Daniel, the translators eliminated from the Cannon for good reason. He still uses some!

Jesus implicitly rejected the Apocrypha as Scripture by referring to the entire recognized Jewish Canon of Scripture. From the blood of Abel (Genesis 4:8) to the blood of Zechariah. (2 Chronicles 24:20) They killed him between the altar and the house of God. "Yes, I tell you," said Jesus, "it shall be charged against this generation." (Luke 11:51, Matthew 23:35)

"The 'oracles of God,' were given to the Jews, (Romans 3:2) and they rejected the Apocrypha as part of the inspired revelation. Interestingly, Jesus had many disputes with the Jews, but He never disputed with them about the extent of the inspired revelation of God. The

105

Apocrypha contains a number of false teachings." – New Advent.

Christian Apologetics Research Ministry claims: "The Apocryphal books do not share many of the characteristics of the Canonical books: they are not prophetic, there is no supernatural confirmation of any of the Apocryphal writers' works, there is no predictive prophecy, there is no new Messianic truth revealed, they are not cited as authoritative by any prophetic book, written after them, and they even acknowledge that there were no prophets in Israel at their time."

He also uses a very weak translation of the Septuagint. Under the title of "The Researchers Library of Ancient Texts," Horn cites this as one of the sources for his proclamations. Horn's own advertisements describe it as being so. "The Septuagint ('Greek Old Testament') is a translation of the Hebrew Old Testament and certain Apocrypha." He openly admits using material not included in the Cannon. This does not seem to concern the multitudes.

Despite the obvious error, he uses both to formulate his so-called prophecies and declarations, adding a Scripture here or there. Because of this he has come out with the most bizarre teachings of our day.

Tom Horn has now placed George H. Pember's book Earth's Earliest Ages, back in print. The book, originally published in 1876, analyzes the prophecy of Jesus Christ in Matthew 24 that says the end times would be a repeat of "the days of Noah." Nothing wrong with that verse in itself, we are living in such times. However, he concludes that the last and most fearful sign heralding the Lord's Second Coming would be the return of the Nephilim mentioned in Genesis 6. Where have we heard all that before other than from the mouth of Francis A. Schaeffer?

Marshall Van Summers is another who claims to be the Messenger for the New Message, another gospel, from God. He said he got his information from angelic beings.

Who and what they are, from Horn's claims, are sheer utter nonsense! Be warned if you are a new believer read on with caution. To coin a phrase I do not want you to become "Hornswoggled."

The enemy is out to deceive! He takes the truth and twists it, and his goal is to see us end up in the fires of hell. We all know he uses television, but when he can weave his way to the front of Christian Television broadcasting he loves it!

He did it through the Hollywood production of the movie Noah! He did it through Jim Bakker, when after his standard Jerry Springer style intro was complete, he hosted Horn. The devil accomplished his goal when Christian TV personality Gary Stearman resigned from his position to join Tom Horn to form SkyWatch TV. Others who have entertained his error through interviews include. Coast to Coast AM, the LA Times Syndicate, ABC, CBS, NBC, CNN, FOX, Time, the New York Times, the Los Angeles Times, Chicago Tribune, Miami Herald, BBC, MSNBC, Michael Savage, SciFi Channel, History Channel, Hannity & Colmes, Sid Roth's "It's Supernatural," Celebration Daystar TV and FaithTV.

Perhaps one of the most earth shattering interviews was with Sid Roth on "It's Supernatural." How was Sid Roth able to become so deceived, to even let him through the door?

In summary, his teachings deal with the Nephilim mentioned in Genesis 6! He says they are creations coming back in our day, the end times, as Aliens carried in UFOs. He claims that these aliens are visiting earth and have a mandate to change our DNA. He further claims that they are supposedly among us as "Watchers." How much further will the church sink before our eyes begin to open? Let's get into the Word of God, my righteous indignation is rising!

"And it came to pass, when men began to multiply on the face of the earth, and daughters were born unto them,

That the sons of God saw the daughters of men that they were fair; and they took them wives of all which they chose." Genesis 6:1-2)

For centuries there has been enormous debate about who these, "sons of God" were. They refer to them as the Nephilim. Some say they were the sons of Seth, who mated with those of the world. Others say they were fallen angels as is the claim of Tom Horn.

His opinion indicates that the "sons of God" were fallen angels (demons) who mated with human women. Jude verse 6, at first glance, may seem to back up this premise.

"And the angels which kept not their first estate, but left their own habitation, he hath reserved in everlasting chains under darkness unto the judgment of the great day."

The pundits of this idea also use Genesis 6:4, to advance their hypothesis.

"There were giants in the earth in those days; and also after that, when the sons of God came in unto the daughters of men, and they bare children to them, the same became mighty men which were of old, men of renown."

Why would demons do such a thing? The Bible does not specifically give us the answer. Demons are evil, twisted beings, so nothing they do should surprise us. As to a distinct motivation, Horn's speculation is that the demons were attempting to pollute the human bloodline to prevent the coming of the Messiah. God had promised that the Messiah would one day crush the head of the serpent, Satan. (Genesis 3:15) The demons in Genesis 6, he claims, attempted to prevent the crushing of the serpent and make it impossible for a sinless "seed of the woman" to be born. Again, this is not a specifically biblical answer, still to some, it's biblically plausible and was partly responsible for the formulation of many opinions around us.

What were the Nephilim? According to Hebraic and other legends (*the Book of Enoch and other non-biblical writings used by Horn*), they were a race of giants and superheroes who did acts of great evil. Their great size and power, they say, came from the mixture of demonic "DNA" with human genetics. According to the movie, Noah, starring Russell Crowe, the Nephilim were fallen angels encased in rock. However, Jude tells us they were bound in darkness in everlasting chains.

Another Scripture that affirms they are bound until the Day of Judgment is:

"For if God spared not the angels that sinned, but cast them down to hell, and delivered them into chains of darkness, to be reserved unto judgment." (2 Peter 2:4)

Right from the outset we can know that for them there is no escape, nor are they coming back. In short, the word everlasting in Jude 6 tells us they are not

109

getting out any time soon. They are bound, yet Horn and others claim they are coming back in the end times. Further, when it comes to such passages of Scripture we need to exercise caution. It is the Christian faith that we believe, profess, propagate, and contend for. We must always be God conscious and never demon conscious!

If we listen to preachers speaking about the Nephilim today, we will discover that they talk for forty-five minutes about UFOs and two minutes about the Lord. Even then, many of them do not even mention the name of Jesus. From this, we can easily determine what spirit they are of. If they direct us to the Lord and not UFOs then they are of God! (1 John 4:2) One thing for sure is that the Nephilim were not aliens, angels, "Watchers," "Guardian Angels" or rock monsters coming from another dimension.

On the surface, some of what their so-called teachings present do sound biblical. It's true that the "sons of God" had sexual relations with the daughters of men. It's true that these "sons of God" took these women as their wives. It's true that God said His spirit will not always strive with man. It's true that God saw the wickedness of man. It's further true that God sighed because he had made man on the earth. (Genesis 6:1-6)

If we are going to determine whether these were fallen angels, we need to examine these six verses in detail. It is also helpful to understand complex words in the light of easier understood words in the same context.

Firstly, let's deal with the rules that the LORD set up for us right in the creation. Seventeen times in the creation Scriptures, the Lord commanded everything and every creature to reproduce after their kind. Why would the LORD have specifically mentioned this term so many times? Did He know that a day would come when we needed to look to those verses to keep us from error? The improper mating of heavenly beings (demons) and earthly women is an attack on the boundaries designed to separate the heavenly and earthly realms. It thus threatens the integrity of creation as God intended it.

First and foremost, the notion that demons can "produce" real bodies and have real sex with real women would invalidate Jesus' argument of the authenticity of His resurrection. Jesus assured His disciples that "a spirit does not have flesh and bones, as you and I have." (Luke 24:39) If indeed a demon could produce flesh and bones, Jesus' argument would not only be flawed, it would be misleading. In fact, it might be logically argued that the disciples did not see the post-resurrection appearances of Christ, rather a demon masquerading as the resurrected Christ.

The Apocryphal books and even some occult books, relied upon by Horn, blatantly attack the integrity of the words of Jesus in Luke 24:39.

The occult world says, "An Incubus is an evil spirit that lies on persons in their sleep; especially one that has sexual intercourse with women while they are sleeping." ERROR! A Succubus they say, "Is a demon assuming female form to have sexual intercourse with men in their sleep." ERROR! The Book of Enoch states that 200 of the Benei Ha'Elohim, (sons of God) decided to marry human women. They were divided into groups of ten, and the leader of each of the ten is named. Notable Watchers. ERROR!

Further regarding the reproduction of demons with humanity, we need to remember that angels neither

111

marry nor are given in marriage (Matthew 22:30; Mark 12:25; and Luke 20:35) Genesis 6:2 says:

"That the sons of God saw the daughters of men that they were fair; and they TOOK THEM WIVES of all which they chose."

Since angels do not marry, the sons of God must not have been angels. The phrase "sons of God" we find mentioned 11 times in Scripture. Six times in the New Testament we find this phrase and each time it refers to the children of God. For instance, John 1:12 says:

"As many as received Him, to them gave He power to become the sons of God, even to them that believe on His name."

Romans 8:14 says: "For as many as are led by the Spirit of God, they are the sons of God."

Horn and others ask: "What happened to the Nephilim?" They say the Nephilim were the primary reason for the great flood in Noah's time. ERROR! Genesis does NOT say that the flood came because of the giants, it came because "God saw that the wickedness of man was great in the earth, and that every imagination of the thoughts of his heart was only evil continually." (Genesis 6:5)

Refusing to accept this correction of Scripture, they try to say that they appeared further on in the Bible. ERROR! In Numbers 13:33, when the spies went into the land they returned with an evil report. They said they saw there the Nephilim, (the sons of Anak) and that they felt very small compared to the size of the Anak. In any event, these "giants" the Israelites destroyed during their invasion of Canaan (Joshua 11:21-22) and later in their history. (Deuteronomy 3:11; 1 Samuel 17) If destroyed, obviously they were not fallen angels, demons! Then, if destroyed, how can they come back as Horn insists?

So who, then, were these Nephilim? Since demons cannot produce offspring of a woman we need to look elsewhere to solve the mystery. Since God saw the sin of man and brought judgment upon man because of the sexual impropriety we must look to the integrity of God. "The LORD, by no means allows the guilty go unpunished." (Nahum 1:3 ERV) The punishment came upon man. Thus, to understand the term "sons of God," we need to shift our focus from demons to man.

Many believe that men of the godly line of Seth took women from the ungodly line of Cain and married them. In the days of Noah, there was a great deal of promiscuity. It overspread the world. However, when the believer intermingled with unbelievers, the LORD put a stop to it. Hence, the words: "The sons of God, (*Sethites*) saw the daughters of men, (*Cainites*) that they were fair; and they took them wives of all which they chose." (Genesis 6:2)

Throughout Scripture, the LORD spoke of His aversion to this and issued stern warnings.

"When the LORD thy God shall bring thee into the land whither thou goest to possess it, and hath cast out many nations before thee, the Hittites, and the Girgashites, and the Amorites, and the Canaanites, and the Perizzites, and the Hivites, and the Jebusites, seven nations greater and mightier than thou;

Neither shalt thou make marriages with them; thy daughter thou shalt not give unto his son, nor his daughter shalt thou take unto thy son.

For they will turn away thy son from following me that they may serve other gods: so will the anger of the

LORD be kindled against you, and destroy thee suddenly." (Deuteronomy 7:1, 3-4)

In another place it tells us:

"And Shechaniah the son of Jehiel, one of the sons of Elam, answered and said unto Ezra, We have trespassed against our God, and have taken strange wives of the people of the land: yet now there is hope in Israel concerning this thing.

Now therefore let us make a covenant with our God to put away all the wives, and such as are born of them, according to the counsel of my lord." (Ezra 10:2-3a)

Horn skillfully in a manipulative way presents his case for the end time return of what he calls, "the Nephilim," using much data from ufologists. People like the occult writer, Erich Von Daniken, "Chariots of the Gods," and Allister Crowley, the most evil man who ever lived in the United Kingdom. He claims that the supposed Nephilim are returning through portals, or star gates. Ninety percent of what he speaks about involves the claimed appearances of UFOs today. Once more he takes truth and weaves a web of the sinister to ensnare people. However, like some spiders at times they get caught in their own web.

Here are his own words: "Unexplained phenomena are occurring all around us, and reports of "beings" trans-versing portals (e.g. ufonauts) are coming in with regular frequency. Whoever or whatever these beings are, the reality of their activity can no longer be doubted."

Nowhere does Jesus even get a mention! Here, lies the essence of his snare. His bait consists of the mysterious seeds of error planted by his words,

114

(ufonauts), and then he backs off as non-committal to allow the seeds of death to grow.

Don't lose your place yet, he gets even more ridiculously unscriptural. On the same website he says:

"The story in 1 Samuel 28 makes reference to the beings that ascended up from 'out of the earth' as 'gods.' (1 Samuel 28.13) When Saul asked the woman with the 'familiar spirit' (1 Samuel 28.7) what had scared her so much, she answered:

"I saw gods ascending out of the earth." (1 Samuel 28.13)

Horn in his own words claims: "The Endorian witch may have identified one of these 'gods' as the deceased Samuel, but many Christians are uncomfortable with the idea of communicating with the dead and insist the reference had to be to something else."

It's so easy for people like this to give a Scripture reference without giving the full words or context of the Scripture. They know that many readers never stop to look up each Bible verse.

Let's set the record straight! Firstly, Saul was dealing with a witch. This woman was possessed by the spirit of divination. There is no way on earth any truth came out of her mouth. Saul asked her to conjure up Samuel. Such in itself is impossible. Jesus said those who are dead, as Samuel was, cannot come back or go anywhere!

"And beside all this, between us and you there is a great gulf fixed: so that they which would pass from hence to you cannot; neither can they pass to us that would come from thence." (Luke 16:26)

Let's read two of those verses in Samuel and see what we can discover.

"And when the woman saw Samuel, she cried with a loud voice: and the woman spake to Saul, saying, Why hast thou deceived me? For thou art Saul.

And the king said unto her, Be not afraid: for what sawest thou? And the woman said unto Saul, I saw gods ascending out of the earth." (1 Samuel 28:12-13)

She was the one, not Saul, who saw what she called Samuel. Saul did not hear any words. She spoke to Saul allegedly relating from Samuel. She was also the one who claimed to have seen these beings ascend. Nothing indicates that Saul had seen anything!

Now let's turn our attention to Horn's statement on the previous page. "Christians are uncomfortable with the idea of communicating with the dead." Indeed, we should run from such a horrid unscriptural thing. The LORD tells us that everything involved in such practices is an abomination in His sight.

"There shall not be found among you any one that maketh his son or his daughter to pass through the fire, or that useth divination, or an observer of times, or an enchanter, or a witch,

Or a charmer, or a consulter with familiar spirits, or a wizard, or a necromancer. (*That's one who supposedly speaks with the dead!*)

For all that do these things are an abomination unto the LORD: and because of these abominations the LORD thy God doth drive them out from before thee. (Deuteronomy 18:10-12)

Of course, these that snare people with this stuff, they had to get it from somewhere else. The common denominator! Could it all come from one single source?

116

YES! They have influenced the Christian church into all kinds of errors. Together, let's follow their trail.

Here is another statement on a Tom Horn related website, quoting a Roman Catholic Professor of Theology.

"Christians will not immediately need to renounce their faith in God 'simply on the basis of the reception of (this) new, unexpected information of a religious character from extraterrestrial civilizations.' However, once the 'religious content' originating from outside the earth 'has been verified' they will have to conduct 'a re-reading (of the Gospel) inclusive of the new data.'" – Vatican Astronomer, Eminent Theologian and Full Professor of Fundamental Theology at the Pontificia Università Della Santa Croce in Rome, (Connected with Opus Dei) Father Giuseppe Tanzella-Nitti.

Did you see that? He is suggesting that in a day ahead people will renounce the faith in the light of Satan's new information!

Only in one place on the entire website does he mention the name of Jesus. No one else referred to mentions the name of Jesus on that site. They speak of a coming of some extraterrestrial Antichrist. They mention nothing about the coming of the Lord! He is, however, relentless in his self-accolades. This, despite the fact that his 7-Fold Vision states:

"Our number one goal now is to share the Gospel of Jesus Christ with millions of people around the world through a fresh and unique paradigm in Christian broadcasting." He is saying he wants to infect the entire world with his error!

In self-praise he announces:

"Following the release of our 2012 best-seller Petrus Romanus: 'The Final Pope is here,' we were inundated with invitations from around the world to be interviewed on radio, television, and in print media. These included segments in The History Channel's 'Countdown to Apocalypse,' which premiered November 9th, 2012; a special feature on Canada's largest Christian channel, VisionTV, titled 'I Prophesy.'"

This book is a tool! Designed to have people discredit it, in the light of his UFO stuff, so that others will not believe the small amounts of truth contained in its pages. Pope Francis may indeed be the last pope! Wanting to draw people's attention from a truth, one hides it in the midst of preposterous error. In this way, people toss the baby out with the bath water!

Look out Canada! He has set his sights on the world! I wonder how many good people he will drag down with him as he gets caught in his own spider web.

A search of his websites reveals that there is nothing mentioned about the coming Kingdom. Not a single word of the gospel is presented. None are given opportunity to accept Jesus Christ as their Savior.

He does promote his books, DVD's, coffee mugs, Tee shirts, Sweatshirts, bumper stickers and even food products. SkyWatch TV – when people click on their preparedness section they are carried to a site that offers gas masks, lights and radios, emergency supplies which include camouflage tents and military cooking utensils. Would you believe it, they also sell K-rations, military survival rations, even gun accessories which include sniper camouflage Ghillie suits. Everything an end of the world cult makes available at exorbitant prices is yours through Tom Horn's SkyWatch TV site.

He also speaks about a retreat center they plan to build on 150 acres of land, free of charge to his followers. (*7-Fold Vision*) Others built such Centers! David Koresh, "the wacko from Waco," who found his end as his military defended compound burned to the ground. Jim Jones was another. There, over 900 Peoples Temple Members committed suicide. Jones made them paranoid about the "outside" world and led them to believe that death (*and "life after death"*) was preferable to whatever fate awaited them.

Thirty nine ended their lives in The Heaven's Gate cult. Cult members who killed themselves believed a spaceship would take them to heaven! Forty eight members of "The Order of the Solar Temple" cult ended their lives, deceived by a form of UFO thinking. In the early 1990s, the concept of transit was introduced in the group. This term they used to describe the voluntary departure of members to another planet in order to create a new world. If you like a new Noah's Ark idea of starting a new world. The group reportedly drew some inspiration for its teachings from British occultist Allister Crowley, who is also cited, by Horn on his site. Who is next?

So, you decide; do you want this man in your church? Have you already heard him on television and become "Hornswoggled" by him?

All of this is Satan designed, to draw away our focus from what is actually taking place in our day! It's time to get our eyes opened to truth. To see the depth of how terribly the common denominator in all of this has tainted and drawn away the church. For this to happen we need to take a fresh look at the prophetic books in the Bible. The hour of the Lord's return is closer than we

119

think. It's time to run to Jesus, the eleventh hour is here! When He comes it will be too late. There are no second chances in that day.

THE BEGINNING OF THE END!

Turning our attention to prophecy as it deals with the end times, every page of Scripture screams a "Final Warning." The reason these prophecies are in the Bible is that He wants us to know clearly what is happening in our day. The newspapers, TV sets, every radio, are all filled with the revealing of Scripture. Syria, Iraq, Iran, Egypt, Afghanistan, North Korea, Russia, I.S.I.S., and the Islamic invasion in the West are all mentioned in the Bible. Everything promised for the end times will come about as an indirect result of a deceived and lukewarm church. One sign of the end is a half-hearted church, brought about by the error of hyper-grace which we discussed. To see how prophecy evolves, we need to go back in history and to the great prophets of the past.

All through Scripture, the prophets declared that God would bring back "the apple of His eye" to the Promised Land. (Jeremiah 33, Zachariah 2:8) This is evolving right before our eyes. Let's recap a Scripture to clear our heads from "The Horn Manifesto."

"Behold, I will send for many fishers, saith the LORD, and they shall fish them; and after will I send for many hunters, and they shall hunt them from every mountain, and from every hill, and out of the holes of the rocks." (Jeremiah 16:16)

We have learned that this Scripture speaks of Israel and describes the rebirth of the nation. There is also, for some, a very frightening aspect of this passage of Scripture. As evangelists stand in their office today, not all will hear their message and some will have to face the consequences. Those who refuse to accept attraction from the hands of loving fishermen will experience the

121

hands of the hunter. The hunters come during the tribulation. Many will be left behind, when the rapture comes. These will be those who seek for anything other than the Jesus of Scripture. They, like the rebellious gentiles upon whom the great delusion comes, will share their lot in a Christ-less eternity. If they only knew what was coming in the days ahead they would run fast and far away from all error. Perhaps this is the reason for "Final Warning!"

A hunter stalks his prey. During the Tribulation, they will seek out half-hearted believers and deliver them up to the tribulation.

"Then shall they deliver you up to be afflicted, and shall kill you: and ye shall be hated of all nations for my name's sake." (Matthew 24:9)

The prophet Zachariah is also given insight into that day and the two witnesses who will stand on the earth at the time of the end!

"And two olive trees by it, one upon the right side of the bowl, and the other upon the left side thereof." (Zachariah 4:3) This perfectly describes the official emblem of Israel today.

The two olive trees represent Joshua and Zerubbabel, whose witness in their day was the prototype of the two witnesses of Revelation 11:3-12. The two olive trees played an important part in the founder's perception of the new State of Israel in 1948, where religion and state and their respective dignitaries (*the high priest and the prime minister*) stand together to realize the Zionist dream, contained in their official emblem.

There has been a great deal of debate about the two witnesses mentioned in the Apocalypse. Some claim

122

they are Moses and Elijah. Others say its Moses and Enoch. Others contend that since Enoch was a gentile it cannot be him. Opponents say that Moses and Enoch would represent the Old and the New Testament saints and that includes the Gentiles. Even as others try to say the witnesses will be two specific messages of the end times. One group says they will be two angels. If left to Tom Horn's error, they would be your local E.T.s. In any event, they will come and may already be on the earth. What will happen to the two witnesses who stand out as pillars of fire in the last days?

"And I will give power unto my two witnesses, and they shall prophesy a thousand two hundred and threescore days, clothed in sackcloth. (*1260 days is 3.45 years not 3.5 years as some claim.*)

These are the two olive trees, and the two candlesticks standing before the God of the earth.

And if any man will hurt them, fire proceedeth out of their mouth, and devoureth their enemies: and if any man will hurt them, he must in this manner be killed.

These have power to shut heaven that it rain not in the days of their prophecy: and have power over waters to turn them to blood, and to smite the earth with all plagues, as often as they will.

And when they shall have finished their testimony, the beast that ascendeth out of the bottomless pit shall make war against them, and shall overcome them, and kill them.

And their dead bodies shall lie in the street of the great city, which spiritually is called Sodom and Egypt, where also our Lord was crucified. (*Notice the mention of Egypt*)

And they of the people and kindreds and tongues and nations shall see their dead bodies three days and an half, and shall not suffer their dead bodies to be put in graves.

And they that dwell upon the earth shall rejoice over them, and make merry, and shall send gifts one to another; because these two prophets tormented them that dwelt on the earth.

And after three days and an half the Spirit of life from God entered into them, and they stood upon their feet; and great fear fell upon them which saw them.

And they heard a great voice from heaven saying unto them, Come up hither. And they ascended up to heaven in a cloud; and their enemies beheld them." (Revelation 11:3-12)

There is nothing new under the sun. (Ecclesiastes 1:9) When a man cannot make another's message ineffective, when they can no longer ignore them, they simply kill them. It happened to Bonhoeffer, it happened to others. It will happen again!

Despite the many uncertainties dealing with these two heroes, there are some things that are sure and set in stone. The words of verse nine speak directly to that certainty.

"And they of the people and kindreds and tongues and nations shall see their dead bodies three days and an half, and shall not suffer their dead bodies to be put in graves."

It says that the whole world looks at their dead bodies. This requires modern telecommunications like satellites and TV to fulfill. Such has not been possible until now, in our technological age.

Another prophecy that could not have been fulfilled until our day! Another revelation that required worldwide telecommunications is found in Luke 21:26.

"Men's hearts failing them for fear, and for looking after those things which are coming on the earth: for the powers of heaven shall be shaken."

At the time this prophecy was given, it could be many months or years before people heard about various disasters. Using word of mouth these disasters would not be seen as the Scripture says. The verse says men's hearts failing them from, "looking" at these disasters. This could only take place through the use of international television.

Matthew 24:22 shows us that if Jesus Christ does not intervene in world affairs, the human race will be faced with extinction.

"And except those days should be shortened, there should no flesh be saved: but for the elect's sake those days shall be shortened."

It's crucial to note that humanity has held the ability for self-annihilation only since the rebirth of Israel in 1948.

When the final hour comes, thousands will cry out to the very mountains to hide them.

"Then shall they begin to say to the mountains, Fall on us; and to the hills, and cover us." (Luke 23:30)

How will it all unfold according with Scripture? How can we know truth from error in our day? The Lord wants us to know His truth! Everything He will do! Everything the enemy will try is clearly given to us in the Word.

The signs of the end are all around us, but the enemy does not want us to know that. This is why he is polluting the world with erroneous end time theologies. He does everything he can to keep the truth from us! He finds no shortage of people to expound his deceit. The clock of grace is ticking and soon will come to a complete stop!

The church needs to abandon so-called manifestations, hyper-grace and all else that waters down truth. We need to embrace the Lord's plumb line, so that we will be able to reach as many precious souls around us as we can before it's too late. (Amos 7:7-9)

"Expensive Grace" is at the opposing end of the spectrum to cheap or hyper-grace. The very presence of cheap-grace is a clear sign that we are on rapid collision course with the end! Before it's too late, we need to cry out to the Lord, "Open my eyes, Lord, show me everything that is coming!" All that is coming has been designed from the very beginning. If your heart is firmly grounded in the love of Christ, there is nothing to fear!

"For God hath not given us the spirit of fear; but of power, and of love, and of a sound mind." (2 Timothy 1:7)

The beginning of the end is long past. It has been with us since 1948 and the birth of Israel. We are racing faster and faster towards the launch of the days of sorrows. (Matthew 24:8)

His love! His mind so filled with peace is ours as we walk through the end times. Through it all, we will trust Jesus more and more. Through it all, we will bask in the cloud of God's presence, not glitter! Through it all, we will depend upon His Word! Through it all, we will thank Him for the mountains and for the valley times! Through it all, we will thank Him for the storms that may come! Storms, He will bring us through as we rest in

126

Him! Only then will we discover what real faith, what real grace can and will do! Then, on that day when we see Him face-to-face, all sorrow will end as He wipes away every tear from our eyes!

NIMROD'S RETURN

Zachariah spelled out to Zerubbabel everything that was to come to Israel and us. There were eight visions presented in his book. The sixth vision we find in chapter five. Remember six is the number of man. In this vision the activity of a man is downplayed, but deals with humanity.

"Then I turned, and lifted up mine eyes, and looked, and behold a flying roll."

And he said unto me, what seest thou? And I answered, I see a flying roll; the length thereof is twenty cubits, and the breadth thereof ten cubits.

Then said he unto me, This is the curse that goeth forth over the face of the whole earth: for every one that stealeth shall be cut off as on this side according to it; and every one that sweareth shall be cut off as on that side according to it." (Zachariah 5:1-3)

The prophet replied to the interpreting angel, who asked him what he saw. A flying scroll that was 30 feet by 15 feet long. The measurements are perhaps only coincidental to the size of the tabernacle and the temple. These were the dimensions of the holy place of the tabernacle (Exodus 26:8) as well as the porch in front of the holy place of Solomon's temple. (1 Kings 6:3)

The scroll that Zechariah saw was open and large so that people could read it easily. During the restoration period, the returnees demonstrated an increased interest in the Mosaic Law, also written on scrolls. (Nehemiah 8) No one could plead ignorance because the scroll in Zachariah's vision was large enough for all to see and read. No one can claim ignorance today because they have the Word of God! Alas, the problem is that some give the Word of the Lord only minutes of their day, relying upon some teacher to tell them what it says. No one has an excuse! The statement, "I was taught in church," won't cut it!

According to what God had previously written in the Law, those who stole and profaned His name would die, thus purging the land of sin. "The time is come that judgment must begin at the house of God." (1 Peter 4:17)

In spite of the glorious promises of the future revealed in the prophet's first visions, the Israelis needed to realize that sin would still bring inevitable divine punishment on them. They needed to remain pure so they could avoid the Lord's curses and enjoy His promised blessings. (2 Corinthians 7:1) Here is the Lord's rule in righteousness! Upon the sea of His righteousness we must sail because once the day of real grace has ended and the day of wrath and judgment is ushered in, with the opening of the seven sealed book of Revelation 5:1-9, there will be no turning back.

The seventh vision brings us closer to our goal. If we do not think that Zachariah's mind was stretched when he saw a flying scroll, let's think again. He was stretched even further by seeing a woman sitting in a basket! Then, two women!

"Then the angel that talked with me went forth, and said unto me, Lift up now thine eyes, and see what, is this that goeth forth.

And I said, what is it? And he said, this is an ephah that goeth forth. He said moreover, this is their resemblance through all the earth.

And, behold, there was lifted up a talent of lead: and this is a woman that sitteth in the midst of the ephah.

And he said, this is wickedness. And he cast it into the midst of the ephah; and he cast the weight of lead upon the mouth thereof.

Then lifted, I up mine eyes, and looked, and, behold, there came out two women, and the wind was in their wings; for they had wings like the wings of a stork: and they lifted up the ephah between the earth and the heaven.

Then said I to the angel that talked with me, whither do these bear the ephah?

And he said unto me, to build it, a house in the land of Shinar: and it shall be established, and set there upon her own base." (Zachariah 5:5-11)

"What is it?" he asked the angel. The basket Zechariah saw is called in Hebrew "hpya'eyphah," a measuring basket which holds a dry measure of quantity, equal to three seahs, 10 omers. It was about the size of a bathtub. It was a basket that held iniquity that had overspread the land. (Zachariah 5:6) The word used, "the resemblance," they translated as iniquity in some ancient versions. In our day, the resemblance, iniquity, counterfeit everything, are flying through the church!

The exiles had returned from Babylon, and their hearts were not right with God, as they carried the sins of the land of Babylon with them into the land of Judah. This is the same as where we stand today. People in our churches come loaded with sin and hurts of the world, where they were held captive. Hurts that have never been totally surrendered. In these last days, the message of total abandonment, of complete surrender of all, must be brought back to the hearts of the people, if our hope is to live again.

The woman in the basket was the personification of sin. In the book of Revelation, we see a similar woman who is called the MOTHER OF HARLOTS. Her name there is "Abominations." Let's read it together.

"And there came one of the seven angels which had the seven vials, and talked with me, saying unto me, Come hither; I will shew unto thee the judgment of the great whore that sitteth upon many waters: With whom the kings of the earth have committed fornication, and the inhabitants of the earth have been made drunk with the wine of her fornication.

So he carried me away in the spirit into the wilderness: and I saw a woman sit upon a scarlet coloured beast, full of names of blasphemy, having seven heads and ten horns.

And the woman was arrayed in purple and scarlet colour, and decked with gold and precious stones and pearls, having a golden cup in her hand full of abominations and filthiness of her fornication:

And upon her forehead was a name written, MYSTERY, BABYLON THE GREAT THE MOTHER OF HARLOTS AND ABOMINATIONS OF THE EARTH." (Revelation 17:1-5)

Who is this "Mother of Abominations?" To properly understand who she is, we need to take a look at the origins of Babylon before we can see her role in the end times.

It's in the following passage of Scripture we discover a demonic oneness which was prophetic of what will be in the days of the Antichrist.

"Cash also had a son named Nimrod, who became a very powerful man on earth.

131

He was a great hunter before the LORD. That is why people compare other men to him and say, 'That man is like Nimrod, a great hunter before the LORD.'

Nimrod's kingdom spread from Babylon to Erech, to Akkad, and then to Calneh, in the land of Babylonia." (Genesis 10:8-10 ERV)

Then, a little further on we read:

"And the whole earth was of one language, and of one speech.

And it came to pass, as they journeyed from the east, that they found a plain in the land of Shinar; and they dwelt there.

And they said one to another, Go to, let us make brick, and burn them throughly. And they had brick for stone, and slime had they for morter.

And they said, Go to, let us build us a city and a tower, whose top may reach unto heaven; and let us make us a name, lest we be scattered abroad upon the face of the whole earth.

And the LORD came down to see the city and the tower, which the children of men builded.

And the LORD said, Behold, the people is one, and they have all one language; and this they begin to do: and now nothing will be restrained from them, which they have imagined to do.

Go to, let us go down, and there confound their language, that they may not understand one another's speech.

So the LORD scattered them abroad from thence upon the face of all the earth: and they left off to build the city." (Genesis 11: 1-8)

Shinar is Babel and later the Babylonian Empire. It included parts of modern-day Turkey, Jordan, Syria,

Egypt, Iraq, Iran, Pakistan and Afghanistan, to name a few. All the countries who today are under attack by Daesh. (I.S.I.S)

Before we look at the Tower of Babel, let's stay with Nimrod. The famous Jewish historian, Josephus, wrote that, "Nimrod used tyranny to threaten the people not to believe in God, but to trust in him and by their own powers prosper."

Tyranny mixed with secular humanism! Secular humanism has tried to invade the church for years. Now has come spiritual humanism. Under the name of "The Church of the Way," their advance in our day is disastrous. Here is what they claim:

"All religions believe in God. Spiritual Humanism accepts the possible existence of God, but we reject being controlled by Lords and Kings. We are a civilized democratic religion. If you want to be worshiped, submit your paperwork, and we will vote on it at our next scheduled meeting." – Spiritual Humanism Church

"If you want to be worshipped," is that not what Nimrod wanted? Nimrod is a picture of the Antichrist. Is this not what Satan wanted when he said: "I will ascend into heaven, I will exalt my throne above the stars of God: I will sit also upon the mount of the congregation, in the sides of the north." (Isaiah 14:13) All that has been will be again! (Ecclesiastes 1:9)

Don't be too surprised if false teachers and false prophets use control, psychological tyranny, to hold us in error. They often convince us that they are the only ones who accurately hear from God. This results in people being convinced that they indeed need their pastor to think for them. In turn, the people lose their confidence in being able to discern the will of God for

133

their lives. They run to them and not to the Lord and the Word of God for their answers! These controllers do as much damage today as Nimrod did back in Genesis. They are dictators who have almost set themselves up as self-styled messiahs!

The deadly trait of narcissistic prophets is that of manipulating believers into thinking "no one else is really preaching the gospel" except that church. Or at least, none is preaching it as effectively as they are! Nimrod was a narcissist of the highest order, controlling everyone around him, holding them with psychological tyranny.

Nimrod built not one, but many cities – Babel, Erech, Accad and Calneh. Nimrod was the first person in the Bible who was referred to as having a kingdom. More significantly, Nimrod was not just the king over a city, he was the emperor over a federation of cities. Here, was the beginning of dictatorship. Today they would have called him a self-styled apostle.

History records that eventually Nimrod was hailed as a son of the sun-god, Bel. (*Aka Marduk*)

Alexander Hislop, in his classic treatise, "The Two Babylon's," revealed that Semiramis claimed to have had a child, Tammuz, by Nimrod sometime after his death. Her child was purportedly a virgin birth. It was here that the cult version of the "Madonna with child" of mythology was birthed. Another counterfeit!

Hislop showed how these ancient myths became the basis for Babylonian worship of Semiramis, later known as Ishtar. This evolved into the Egyptian story of the goddess Isis, and the Grecian and Roman goddesses, Venus, Diana, and Athena. Notice again the reference to the name, Isis, or today, Daesh, I.S.I.S.

The mystery thickens! Turning our attention to the Tower of Babel, some amazing truths begin to come to light.

"And they said, Go to, let us build us a city and a tower, whose top may reach unto heaven; and let us make us a name, lest we be scattered abroad upon the face of the whole earth.

And the LORD came down to see the city and the tower, which the children of men builded.

And the LORD said, Behold, the people is one, and they have all one language; and this they begin to do: and now nothing will be restrained from them, which they have imagined to do." Genesis 11: 4-6)

For a moment, let's accept the possibility that there exists a prophetic aspect to the story of Nimrod. Notice in verse six, the LORD said that because of their oneness, nothing would be restrained from them. These limitless possibilities will be the opposing forces to the unity of true believers in the last days. Would this be the Ecumenical Movement or even something more sinister among evangelicals? Just as we live and move and have our being in Jesus so they will in like manner dwell in Satan. Perhaps unknowingly!

The name of the tower was: "Migdal-el." It means tower or gate of God. Some have even described it as an open door to heaven. The conclusion is, Babel and Babylon are cited by varying and many sources to mean the replacement of the gate of heaven. It represents a counterfeit means of entering through a door to glory. In this it references the Antichrist. Jesus said: "I am the gate; whoever enters through me will be saved. They will come in and go out, and find pasture." (John 10:9)

Remember the aim of Nimrod was to enter or experience heaven by another way. It was not some astrological observatory they built. Nor was it some star gate through which the Nephilim led by Nimrod will return, as Horn suggests.

Their demonic oneness mentioned should begin to open our eyes to know that the New Age and many others are again building their tower of oneness in our day. Churches, where they seek the manifestation and not the Manifestor, in their gathering storm of demonic oneness demote God and deify man. Bethel in Redding, California is well known for this. It's a tower that is overspreading the church. Jesus said in Matthew 7: 13-14)

"Enter ye in at the strait gate: for wide is the gate, and broad is the way, that leadeth to destruction, and many there be which go in thereat.

Because strait is the gate, and narrow is the way, which leadeth unto life, and few there be that find it."

The destruction of the wide gate, the counterfeit, Babel/Babylon that came upon them in days passed, so awaits many in the future. The LORD, who knows the end from the beginning, resolved the issue before it arrives in the future.

No, they will not build a physical tower! Horn suggests that the Roman Catholics built a tower, a portal through which entities from another dimension come. Nimrod's tower of the end times will be much more advanced than that. Perhaps it will be some deep spiritual teachings. The gospel age is ending with one final, concerted, all-encompassing onslaught against those who bear witness to and earnestly contend for the faith. (Jude 3) They will also use science, psychology, paranormal activity, materializations, spirit writing and cultism as they come together in an evil oneness, awaiting the rise of the Antichrist.

The founder of Babylon, his wife was the first called "the mother of abominations" and "the Queen (or mother) of heaven."

Back to the book of Revelation! The angel told John that this Harlot, the false religious system, would have as its main teachings the same occult practices as did ancient Babylon. (Revelation 17) It would include black magic, demon contact, séances, miraculous materializations (*perhaps, golden glitter, jewels, orbs of light, angel feathers or spirit writing*), witchcraft, astrology and sorcery. We know that the ancient city of Babylon was ruled by these occult influences. What is not generally known is that the religion of Babylon passed from empire to empire until the days of ancient Rome. The Nimrod clan was the very first apostate church in the history of man! He and the Queen of heaven, they have returned!

"BATTLE FOR TRUTH"

John's desire in Revelation was for us, his readers, to understand that a religious Babylon would be revived to control the last great world power in the last days of history. This is what is meant by the words in verse 11 of Revelation 17: "the beast that was, and is not, and yet is." The Wisdom of Solomon also reminds us again that there is nothing new under the sun. (Ecclesiastes 1:9) He told us that what was, is yet to come!

Babylon existed for a time, then seemed to die out only to come again! It will have great power and influence over the revived Roman Empire and its leader, the Antichrist.

John's desire was to help us know the enemy's tactics and how we can win the battle for truth in the end times! The goal of all prophets was to have us understand how everything will come together at the time of the end.

Back in Zechariah, he saw: "two women, and the wind was in their wings; for they had wings like the wings of a stork: and they lifted up the ephah between the earth and the heaven." (Zachariah 5:9) We are told in Jeremiah 8:7 that: "the stork in the heaven knoweth her appointed times."

It's normal and traditional for storks to leave western and mid Europe in August in what they consider one of the most spectacular migratory flights in the world.

"Over a quarter million storks fly in clouds over the city of Istanbul in Turkey during the course of a few weeks. Their main nesting place in the Middle East is Egypt and Iraq. The stork is well known for returning to a previously used nest. Egypt and Iraq are the nest of Babylon." (The New Cruse – Pentecostal Pioneers.org)

In the words of Augustine: "Babylon is a former Rome, and Rome a, later Babylon; Rome is a daughter of Babylon."

The two Babylons' are contrasted in chapters seventeen and eighteen of Revelation. The Babylon of chapter seventeen is symbolic of Rome; it is mystic Babylon.

As we continue to join the spiritual dots we make a discovery! "Where are they taking the basket?" Zechariah asks. "To the country of Babylon," the angel replies! "To build a house for it." Literally to the plains of Shinar, the location in ancient Mesopotamia of the city of Babylon. "When it's ready, the basket will be set there in its place." (Zachariah. 5:5-11)

Alright, we know where it was going to, but we need to isolate from where the journey will originate in the last days. The long journey of the stork originates from their home in mid Europe, which includes Rome!

According to scholars, the woman in Zachariah's basket is the woman of Revelation 17, Rome! At the end of the age, the religious system currently headquartered in Rome will return to Babylon from where it came. There it will be absorbed into the one world religion, one world government, of the Antichrist. This will bring the world's political, commercial, and religious power together under one central authority. This is the house the angel told Zachariah that they will build.

Has the building begun? Recently Russian troops massed on the Ukrainian borders. This followed the Russian annexation of the Crimea. Putin met with the leader of China and he supports missiles in Iran. Russia is part and parcel of the Gog Magog Alliance of the end times and they will align with the beast! (Ezekiel 38, 39) In fact, Magog, translated by Bible Commentators is none other than Russia. As you read this, Russia by invitation has their troops flowing into Syria in open defiance of the Allies. Theirs will be a coalition of hell as they position themselves on the borders of Israel. Iran on the other hand is a central key player of the alliance and will take its lead from Russia.

The United States of America just entered into an agreement with Iran, lifting sanctions and giving a green light to the development of nuclear power. Of course, the leaders of that nation promise they will not develop nuclear weapons. Can they be trusted? Will the Congress of the United States be able to stop this agreement? I don't think so! The prophet Isaiah spoke specifically about this covenant with death.

"Wherefore hear the word of the LORD, ye scornful men that rule this people which is in Jerusalem.

Because ye have said, we have made a covenant with death, and with hell are we at agreement. (Isaiah 28: 14:15a)

Then, just a few verses later, it says:

"And your covenant with death shall be disannulled, and your agreement with hell shall not stand; when the overflowing scourge shall pass through, then ye shall be trodden down by it." (Isaiah 28: 18)

Will stopping it avert the world from being plunged into a massive war? Who will stop it? What will be the role of the United States in the scheme of things in the days ahead? You decide!

Another member of the gathering military confederacy is Kim Jong-un of North Korea. Russia and

North Korea have an integrated railway line linking them to South Korea, Iran, Syria and Egypt. The Pan Asian line funded and being built will bring South East Asian economies closer to China. This will also militarily link them with Russia, North Korea, Iran and Syria and Egypt. From there they will be able to come down the northern highway and stand against Israel in their millions. (Ezekiel 38)

Daesh, I.S.I.S (*Islamic State of Iraq in Syria*), an Al-Qaeda offshoot based in Syria, first launched an offensive within the borders of Iraq and Syria and now Egypt. All three are part of the once Mesopotamia. Isis, as we learned, was a pagan deity worshiped by those countries and connects to Bel as mentioned in the book of Daniel. They eventually referred to her as the Queen of heaven. That reminds us again of Nimrod's wife who was also called by the same name. Today a resurgence of Isis worship is under way, especially in Kermetic Wicca, which is rampant in our nations.

Obviously, the use of the name, I.S.I.S., is clearly spiritual. Daesh (*I.S.I.S.*) has also declared themselves the caliphate, meaning they are the direct descendants of Muhammad. Caliphate comes from the word Khalif, meaning succession. In short, they are centering control of all Islam back to Iraq, Iran, Syria, Egypt, and Turkey the once Babylonian empire. Let's go back for a second to the flight of the stork and a reminder from chapter one.

In recent months, the Pope convened a Prayer Peace Summit with Israel and the Palestinian Authority. Also in attendance at that meeting was Syria and the Patriarch of Constantinople, Turkey. Where did that take place? The Vatican, of course! Immediately following this summit, the Pope stabbed Israel in the back!

In recent weeks, the Pope has come out and recognized Palestine as a state. This statement is a direct attempt to disenfranchise the Jewish people. Meeting with Palestinian officials at the Vatican, church officials agreed to formally recognize the "State of Palestine" as part of a deal concerning Catholic activities in the Palestinian-controlled areas. This outrageous step was a severe blow to Catholic-Jewish relations and it cannot go unanswered by Israel. Nor can it go unanswered by the Bible believing church! It will certainly not go unanswered by the Lord! It was also prophetic of the betrayal that the Antichrist will bring halfway through the tribulation.

In biblical terms, by recognizing a Palestinian State in Judea and Samaria, the Vatican is effectively seeking to deny the eternal covenant between God and the Jewish people, to whom this land was given long ago. At the same time, the Pope's counterpart, the Coptic Pope, said this regarding Israel.

"Do not believe their claims that they are God's chosen people because it is not true." - Wikipedia

Will there come a demonic oneness between the 1.2 billion Roman Catholic followers and the 18 million Coptic followers? Since the Coptic Church finds its headquarters in Egypt, will this be the political attraction for Rome to move its diplomatic H.Q. there while the Pope himself moves to Shinar?

"The Babylon Fortress was an ancient fortress city or a castle in the Delta of Egypt, located in Babylon in the area today known as Coptic Cairo!" -Wikipedia

This is the residence of the Coptic pope! Could this be the landing of the stork? (Zachariah 5:1)

Revelation 17 and 18 says that, in the last days, Rome will become a world political power, just like the Roman Empire of old. This is why we see the Pope, who is a religious figure, suddenly getting very involved with movements and causes as a political figure. He and his opinions (*Papal Encyclical*) on climate change were recognized and hailed by Ban Ki-moon, Secretary General of the United Nations.

It's been reported that this Papal Encyclical was leaked to the media, and it also contains a call to the UN for the establishment of a one world religion with the papacy at its head. The beast rises and the stork of Zachariah is in flight as Babylon re-assembles!

Again, Revelation presents two aspects of Babylon in chapter 17. There is a spiritual Babylon, corrupting the world with sin through religion. For this reason, she is called "Mystery" because she uses religion to deceive the world and lead people astray. Don't think for one minute that this corruption is isolated to Roman Catholicism. It was its birthplace! In 1962, under Vatican II, the Catholic Charismatic Movement was endorsed by Pope John the 23rd. Since then they have experienced all sorts of so-called manifestations in churches.

Michael Freze in his book, "Voices, Visions and Apparitions," says: "On June 24th, 1987, one lady stated that her rosary had turned gold while she was visiting Medjugorje. (*A major Marian site they visit*) This same woman claims that over a fourth of the people whom she ministered to have had their rosaries turned to gold. This phenomenon is not at all unusual, thousands have come back from Medjugorje testifying that their rosaries turned to gold, the chain or beads often turn to gold immediately during a prayer service in the presence of hundreds of witnesses." (*Page 61*)

"In Conyers, Georgia, gold dust has also been seen upon the worshippers of Mary. There are signs in the sun that accompany this gold phenomena, making the link between gold and the sun too obvious to miss. A study of Roman Catholicism's occult symbols and relics reveal worship of the sun-god who is also worshipped today in different guises by Free Masonry, Illuminist groups, false religions and cults. Isis with her sun symbol and crown upon her head!" - Jeannette Haley

At the Sainte-Anne-de-Beaupré Shrine in Quebec, Canada, orbs of light have been the manifestation for years. When asked about it, they claim: "Our Lord is working great marvels in favor of the holy mother of the Most Blessed Virgin Mary."

Who or what is Saint Anne? Their website gives the answer. "Even if we know very little about the life of Saint Anne, the simple fact of being the mother of Mary and the grandmother of Jesus, is sufficient for the Church to recognize and worship her for centuries."

In other places in Roman Catholicism, orbs of light have been interpreted as angels. In the Cherubic Hymn of the Byzantine Liturgy the Archangels Michael, Gabriel, and Raphael are invoked, as well as our Guardian Angels. Will this be the next step for people in the renewal centers? Attending, hoping to drum up these orbs of light.

Another group of Roman Catholics hold seminars dealing with angels. Not the Lord, but angels and angel feathers! Here is a quote from one of them.

"White feathers may appear in the most unlikely places. When you have found a white feather, carry it round with you to keep your angel close. Once, when I was teaching an angel seminar, I mentioned that white feathers are a common angel sign. After the seminar a woman said that, despite what she had heard, she was not convinced of the existence of angels. At that very moment another student noticed a pure white feather stuck to the sleeve of her cardigan."

Looks like Solomon was right when he said there is nothing new. I wonder what else we can discover in Rome long before it ever infected the renewal churches.

The Bethel church in Redding, California, allegedly introduced soaking prayer, but they were not the first out of the gate with this. The Roman Catholics taught it for generations under the name of "prayer of quiet," practiced by Catholic saints while stroking the rosary. Where did Todd Bentley, Bill Johnson, "Catch the Fire," or "The Elijah List," come by it? Certainly not through some new revelation as some claim.

Even more of these so-called manifestations are found in Roman Catholicism. Spirit writing or automatic writing is at home there. Vassula Rydén has claimed to be receiving new, private revelations, dictated by an entity which she identifies with Jesus. The contents of the revelations refer essentially to the ecumenical movement, the Hearts of Jesus and Mary, the conversion of both humanity and the Church. The product of this spirit writing has been acknowledged and hailed by both bishops and cardinals alike.

All this occurred long before it happened in Neo-Pentecostal churches around the world. In Bethel at Redding, California, the incubator of error, their manifestations started in October of 2011. What negative influence has the Roman Church and Mary worship had on the church today?

The attack on the church of Jesus Christ has been relentless. Joel described our day with these words.

"The leavings of the caterpillar has the locust eaten, and the leavings of the locust has the palmerworm eaten, and the leavings of the palmerworm has the cankerworm eaten." (Joel 1:4) He describes the frightening destruction of what once were the lush green fields (*lives*) of the church. (1 Corinthians 3:9 LITV)

The "gnawing locust" implies chewing and feeding on the crops - the lush green pastures of the church, designed for our rest. (*Gold dust, angel feathers, orbs of light, Backmasked worship*) The harvest has been destroyed by the gnawing and cutting of the locust. (*Manifestations sought as opposed to evangelism's harvest*) Whatever crops are left over are eaten by the "swarming locust." The term "swarming" indicates an enormous and uncontrollable infestation. (*Sozo with their phenomenal growth*) Next comes the "creeping locust"; the term "creeping" refers to a licking action. This implies that all moisture is sucked out and absorbed. (*Hyper-grace, abandoning of the word and Prophetic Prayer*) The nation is left dry and desolate. (*A drought of the real Word*) When one would expect that nothing more could be taken, the "stripping locust" arrives and devours every last blade of grass, every ounce of grain until there is absolutely nothing left over. (*Horn's ridiculous and Romanism*) Their target: the harvest, the precious fruit of the earth. (James 5:7) All have done immense damage while the church slept!

"He hath laid my vine waste, and barked my fig tree: he hath made it clean bare, and cast it away; the branches thereof are made white." (Joel 1:7) The heart of The Father breaks in those words as He longs for His babies to come home. Everything in Joel is prophetic of the end times. The locust plague is just the beginning, a small taste of the future events to come. In our day history is repeating itself.

Let's go back to Conyers, Georgia, where gold dust has been seen upon the worshippers of Mary. They claimed that "these are signs in the sun that accompany the gold phenomena, making the link between gold and the sun too obvious to miss." Isis, the sun god!

For generations, popes including Francis, in ceremonies, hold up an ancient symbol. It is a symbol of the sun god that is carried on a piece of gold formed like a crescent moon. In ancient Egypt this symbolic representation was that of the mother of gods, Isis!

If we take a look at the Islamic crescent moon on top of any mosque at sunrise or sunset the similarity is shocking. If we look at a figurine of Isis, the wife of the sun god and Mother of the gods, it is the same thing carried on top of a crescent moon by the Pope. The very same image can be found in a nine foot tall image of the Catholic Mary in a church in Chicago Illinois.

"Mary, (*Mariam in Arabic*) the mother of Jesus (*Isa*) is considered one of the most righteous women in the Islamic tradition. She is mentioned more in the Quran than in the entire New Testament and is also the only woman mentioned by name in the Quran." - Wikipedia

"The Roman Catholic Marian Bible" states: "Even the infidel, Muhammad glorifies Mary in his Koran, saying, the angels shall say to Maryam, Allah has chosen thee; he has made thee exempt from all stain."

Without stain means to be without sin!

The papacy has in years past listed Mary as a co-redemptrix with Christ. This means she is as much the Savior as Jesus! Digging a little deeper we discover, other heresies of Rome.

"Among Roman Catholics, the Madonna is recognized not only as the mother of God, but also, according to modern Popes, as the Queen of the Universe, Queen of heaven, Seat of Wisdom, and even the Spouse of the Holy Spirit." - Time Magazine, "Handmaid or Feminist." December 30, 1991, p. 62-66

"The truth of the Assumption, defined by Pius XII, is reaffirmed by the Second Vatican Council, which thus expresses the Church's faith: Mary was preserved free from all guilt of original sin, the Immaculate Virgin was taken up body and soul into heavenly glory upon the completion of her earthly sojourn. She was exalted by the Lord as Queen of the Universe...For the mother of Christ is glorified as 'Queen of the Universe.'" Pope John Paul II, Redemptoris Mater (On the Blessed Virgin Mary in the Life of the Pilgrim Church), Encyclical promulgated on 03-25-1987, #41.

Most Roman Catholic adherents cheerfully refer to the Virgin Mary as the Queen of heaven and understand this term as one of endearment, love, and adoration. "The Queen of heaven!" That reminds us again of Nimrod's wife who was also called by the same name. Be warned as we read this Scripture the term for Mary, "Queen of heaven," is not something new.

"The children gather wood, and the fathers kindle the fire, and the women knead their dough, to make cakes to the queen of heaven, and to pour out drink offerings unto other gods, that they may provoke me to anger." (Jeremiah 7:18)

Do Roman Catholics today not worship Mary?

Let's see if we can identify Rome and her popes with more clarity. Who does the book of Revelation speak of when it mentions the number 666?

"Here is wisdom. Let him that hath understanding count the number of the beast: for it is the number of a man; and his number is Six hundred threescore and six." (Revelation 13:18)

The first clue in our pursuit is that he is a man who carries the number 666. He is the son of perdition, meaning the son of Satan. The Bible tells us to count the number for it is the number of a man. Latin, Greek, and Hebrew have numerical values assigned to various letters in their alphabets. When one looks at the names carried by the Papacy something eye opening jumps out at us. One of the titles used by popes is "Vicar of Christ," or vicar of the Son of God. In Latin it is: "Vicarius Filii Dei."

When we take a look at the numerical values of this title it adds up to 666. That in itself is not proof beyond reasonable doubt that the Papacy is the beast. It does, however, open the door for further investigation and presents us with a decision to make.

"Let no man deceive you by any means: for that day shall not come, except there come a falling away first, and that man of sin be revealed, the son of perdition;

Who opposeth and exalteth himself above all that is called God, or that is worshipped; so that he as God sitteth in the temple of God, shewing himself that he is God." (2Thesselonians 2:3)

Just what if someone already sits in a temple proclaiming himself to be God? What if someone were already here who could hold influence over the Islamic nations and Israel? We have already seen how Francis is rising on the political stage of the world. What if the apostate church were already in the world? The word Antichrist doesn't just mean against Christ, it means "in place of Christ." As mentioned the Pope is called the Vicar of Christ.

According to the unabridged "Webster New Twentieth Century Dictionary," the word "vicar" means "a person who acts in the place of another." Are we getting closer to identifying the son of perdition? I am not saying that Pope Francis is the Antichrist. However, I am saying that he claims to be the replacement of Christ. You must decide! The trumpets of "Final Warning" are blowing! Here is what some others have said throughout the years.

Pope Pius IX said, "I alone... am the successor of the apostles, the vicar of Jesus Christ. I am the way, the truth, and the life..." - Pope Pius IX, History of the Christian Church, by Henry Charles Sheldon, p. 59.

Pope Pius X declared, "The Pope is not simply the representative of Jesus Christ. On the contrary, he is Jesus Christ Himself, under the veil of the flesh. Does the Pope speak? It is Jesus Christ who is speaking, hence, when anyone speaks of the Pope, it is not necessary to examine but to obey." - Pope Pius X, Evangelical Christendom, Vol. 49, January 1st, 1895 A.D., p. 15, "the organ of the Evangelical Alliance," published in London by J. S. Phillips.

Pope Pius XII said, "...recognize the Holy, Roman Church to be the only true Church of Jesus Christ,

150

outside which neither sanctity nor salvation can be found. Call them to the unity of one fold, granting them the grace to believe every truth of our holy faith and to submit themselves to the Supreme Roman Pontiff, the Vicar of Jesus Christ on earth." - Pope Pius XII, the Raccolta, Benzinger Brothers, Boston, 1957 A.D., No. 626.

Ah, the demonic oneness of Nimrod has returned!

These blasphemous Papal proclamations oppose what Jesus told us in John 14:6, "I am the way, the truth, and the life: no man cometh unto the Father, but by me."

None of these proclamations have been rescinded or recanted of by the Vatican to this day. In accordance with Papal law, they remain as good today as the day they were announced.

Let the battle for truth be engaged in every church around the globe! The common denominator, the source of the error infesting the churches today with glittery gold dust, orbs of light and a hundred other things is here being isolated and exposed! It's Rome!

FINAL WARNING

The second Babylon is an economic Babylon, which through commerce pollutes the world with material goods. We need to understand what is taking place in the nations of our day in the realm of commerce and religion. The Chinese markets crumbled, affecting nations all around the globe. For a time, that plummet was stabilized. How will it end? These birth pangs in commerce will continue with greater intensity. One day, investors will feel an internal rest, in a time of prosperity, then sudden destruction will come, as a woman in travail. (1 Thessalonians 5:3) At that time, will Babylon, Rome, come to the aid of the world with their massive stockpile of cash? The stock markets race towards the greatest crash in the history of humanity!

"And he cried mightily with a strong voice, saying, Babylon the great is fallen, is fallen, and is become the habitation of devils, and the hold of every foul spirit, and a cage of every unclean and hateful bird.

For all nations have drunk of the wine of the wrath of her fornication, and the kings of the earth have committed fornication with her, and the merchants of the earth are waxed rich through the abundance of her delicacies.

And I heard another voice from heaven, saying, Come out of her, my people, that ye be not partakers of her sins, and that ye receive not of her plagues.

For her sins have reached unto heaven, and God hath remembered her iniquities." (Revelation 18:2-5)

At last we get a real glimpse of the power and influence of Rome in the last days. She is the habitation of demons and every foul spirit known to humanity.

Everything that is unclean lies within her doors, not just child molestation that was covered by her church hierarchy.

All the nations of the resurgent Roman Empire shall wallow in her pagan ways, getting drunk together, and perhaps later, drunk on the blood of the martyrs. (Revelation 17:6) The kings of the earth will commit fornication with her, seduced by the words of her mouth. Has this already begun through the kings of the earth? We are to rule and reign with Jesus as Kings on the earth. (Revelation 5:10) Have we sold this away to seductive words? The church has embraced her deceptions of manifestations? Will we also join with her in idolatrous worship and finally worship of Mary?

Cultural Roman Catholic countries already encourage their subjects to embrace all of Rome. The merchants of the world who will find riches through her one world currency are in for a shock. Today the vastness of the wealth of the Vatican is staggering. This economic power is what's referred to as "her delicacies." (Revelation 18:3) In time, they will say, "Oh, how the mighty have fallen!"

When the economic collapse comes, the world will be plunged into war. In 1967, a book entitled "Report from Iron Mountain" was released. The report was the culmination of the gathering of world leaders in Iron Mountain, U.S.A. Their topic of discussion was "Is world lasting peace possible?" Naturally, their conclusion was no! This determination led them into further discussion. Since World War II brought the world out of the depression following the stock market crash of the 20's, they agreed to take steps to balance the markets. These world leaders agreed that when necessary, the use of

153

military conflict, nationally or internationally would bring the world out of another crisis. Since then, we have seen military conflicts around the world do exactly that. In every nation affected by war, their economies surged as money was poured into their coffers. Building projects, homes, businesses, factories, government buildings, all infrastructure, stimulated the economies, bringing those nations back from the edge.

Nearly all wars are fought over control of territory, and sometimes over specific economic resources such as minerals, oil, farmland, or cities. The patterns of victory and defeat in wars through history have shaped the world's economic direction and its institutions. Vietnam, The Falklands, Ulster, Bosnia, Iraq, Afghanistan, Crimea, Ukraine, and Syria just to name a few, benefited economically from war. While the soldiers fought and died, they knew little of what was really behind the conflict. When the end times stock market crashes, war will again break out as the Antichrist gains control.

Before we turn our attention to the glorious eighth and final vision of Zachariah, let's take a look at another eight. Let's further identify beyond any reasonable doubt that Rome is the headquarters of darkness in these last days.

To everything the Lord brings about at the time of the end, the enemy will try in similitude to have things his way. The eight visions of Zachariah bring us back to the intriguing words of Revelation 17:10-11.

"And there are seven kings: five are fallen, and one is, and the other is not yet come; and when he cometh, he must continue a short space.

And the beast that was, and is not, even he is the eighth, and is of the seven, and goeth into perdition."

To gain a fuller understanding of existing prophecy dealing with these eight kings, we need to travel back in time to my native County Down in Northern Ireland. As we go, we must know that everyone who rises to the papacy is declared the king of Vatican City and since Pius IX they are pronounced infallible. Without sin! There is only one without sin! Jesus! (Hebrews 4:15) Not the Pope!

Bishop St. Malachy, (1094-1148) served as bishop of Connor, then Down, and finally as the Archbishop of Armagh, all in Northern Ireland. Many claim that St. Malachy predicted the final 112 popes beginning with Pope Celestine II (*elected in 1143*), not by name, but by a short epithet, or motto for each, leading us to the final pope before the Apocalypse, who many claim is none other than Pope Francis. Listen to Malachy's final words.

"In the final days of the Holy Roman Church there will reign Peter the Roman, who will feed his flock, among many tribulations; after which the seven hilled city (*Rome, the seat of the Vatican*) will be destroyed and the dreadful Judge will judge the people." – Malachy Prophecies (*Paraphrased for length*)

It is striking that at least one other pope had a similar revelation:

In 1909, while granting an audience, Pope Pius X leaned back and closed his eyes. Suddenly he "awoke" and cried out: "What I see is terrifying. Will it be myself? Will it be my successor? What is certain is that the pope will quit Rome, and in leaving the Vatican, he will have to walk over the dead bodies of his priests."

Will this be the flight of the stork?

Let's look at the last eight of Malachy's prophesied popes!

"The Burning Fire." PIUS X. 1903-1914. This Pope showed a burning passion for spiritual renewal in the Church.

"An Angelic Shepherd." PIUS XII. 1939-1958. This Pope had an affinity for the spiritual world and received visions which have not been made public. Some claim that Pius XII emerged as one of the great popes of all time, and that he was in the truest sense of the word an Angelic Pastor to the flock.

"Pastor and Mariner." JOHN XXIII. 1958-1963. John was known as a pastor to the world, much beloved, and the Patriarch of Venice. Venice the city of gondolas, boats. The connection to "mariner" is remarkable.

"Flower of Flowers." PAUL VI. 1963-1978. Paul's coat-of-arms depicts three fleurs-de-lis, corresponding to Malachy's prophecy. His coat of arms included three flowers. *(Iris blossoms)*

"Of the Half-Moon." JOHN PAUL I. 1978-1978. John Paul was elected Pope on August 26th, 1978, when there was a half-moon. It was in its waning phase when he died the following month, soon after an eclipse of the moon. He reigned 33 days, about one month, when he died, although many believe he was murdered. Was John Paul I the king referred to as "When he comes, he will stay, only a short time." (Revelation 17:10)

"The Labor of the Son." JOHN PAUL II. 1978-2005. Pope John Paul II was the most traveled Pope in history. He circled the globe numerous times, preaching to huge audiences everywhere he went. He survived an assassination attempt. Like the sun, which never ceases to labor and provides light daily. This Pope was

156

incessant. He was born on May 18th, 1920. On that date in the morning there was a near total eclipse of the sun over Europe. This 110th Pope was "De Labore Solis." (*Of the Solar Eclipse, or, From the Toil of the Sun*) Like the sun he came out of the East. (Poland)

Next came "The Glory of the Olive." Benedict XVI. The Order of St. Benedict has said this Pope will come from their order. It is interesting that Jesus gave his apocalyptic prophecy about the end of time from the Mount of Olives.

Malachy's 111th prophesy is none other than "Gloria Olivae" (*The Glory of the Olive*). Saint Benedict himself prophesied that before the end of the world his order, known also as the Olivetans, will triumphantly lead the Catholic Church in its fight against evil. Pope Benedict XVI retired. Is he the one in Revelation 17, described as he "who is"? He is still alive!

"Peter the Roman." This final Pope may be the Antichrist, taking the form of a man named Peter who will gain a worldwide allegiance and adoration. He may be the Antichrist, of whom prophecy foretold. The 112th of Malachy's prophesies states: "There will reign Petrus Romanus, who will feed his flock amid many tribulations; after which the seven-hilled city will be destroyed and the dreadful Judge will judge the people. The End." Malachy's prophecies ended there!

Is Francis this Peter of Rome? Will there come yet another? Are Malachy's prophecies the reason that there has never been a pope elected from Ireland? After all, Ireland was the home of the whistleblower! Just like any other deception the last pope will not come out openly using the name Peter of Rome. The prophecies of

Malachy assure us of that fact. The name will be concealed in one way or another!

Jorge Mario Bergoglio, (*Pope Francis*) was an Argentine cardinal of the Roman Catholic Church. As the Archbishop of Buenos Aires, he served since 1998. He was elevated to the cardinalate in 2001. Pope Francis the 1st took his name in honor of Saint Francis of Assisi, an Italian Catholic friar and preacher (*and Catholic Saint*) who worked with the poor and who established both the Franciscan order for men, and the Order of St. Clare for women.

Something that may play into this, which has also been overlooked by many, is the fact that Francis of Assisi was born in Italy. In addition, he was a Roman priest/friar whose real name was Giovanni di Pietro (*Peter*) di Bernardone, who was nicknamed, Francesco. Some believe this translates literally to "Peter the Roman."

One hundred and twelve popes, Malachy declared would come. If he was correct in the first 111, can he be wrong when it comes to the 112th? Of course he could be wrong. Francis or not, in any event the satanic eight of Revelation 17, all from within the same line of doctrinal error, will come to pass according to God's timing. Verse 11 of John's narrative assures us they will all come from the same line of error. "He is the eighth, and is of the seven."

Now we turn our attention back to the eighth vision of Zachariah. Eight is the number of new beginnings. Stepping once more into the supernatural, the prophet sees four chariots coming out of two bronze mountains. (Zachariah 6:1-8) Common sense requires us to ask: why would the Lord show the prophet things that to us seem so difficult to understand. The answer is simple. The Lord showed him nothing that was not explained. Zachariah also knew the prophecies of former generations. Jesus also said: "Unto you it is given to know the mystery of the kingdom of God: but unto them that are without, all these things are done in parables." (Mark 4:11)

God will not say or do anything that is not already in His word. The Bible is our final authority, designed to keep us from deception. Everything in the New Testament is in the Old Testament concealed, and all in the Old is in the New revealed. Why are ministries today trying to get people to abandon the written Word and seek some new revelation?

Mountains in the Old Testament represent immovability. Something that cannot be moved, naturally, by the hand of man. Perhaps these two mountains represent the sovereignty and righteousness of God. It is the immovable sovereignty of God upon which all kingdoms rise and fall. It is in righteousness, He will judge the world. (Acts 17:31) It's into our world these chariots will ride.

The angel shows to all of us how the end will come, through the colors of the horses involved. It has been suggested that the colors represent: red = war and bloodshed, black = death, white = triumph, and dappled = pestilence. He then explains that these are four spirits that came from the presence of the Lord. Here is God's permissive will, brought about by the choices of man!

We know from many other Scripture references that this is exactly how the end will come. First, economies will tumble and famines will be reported all over the world. (Matthew 24:7) It's happening today!

Sickness, epidemics are loosed on every hand! (Matthew 24:7) Ebola, Middle East respiratory syndrome, Anthrax, HIV/Aids, Bird Flu, and at least one case of the Black Death which was just recently reported in the U.S.A.

Then, will come wars and then more wars and earthquakes in different places! (Mark 13:8) Wikipedia reports, "In the 15th century there were 29 wars, 16th century 59 wars, 17th century 75 wars, 18th century, 69 wars, 19th century 294 wars and the 20th century 278 wars." Currently, daily reported deaths by military conflict around the globe are soaring. Half the world is already at war and the other half can't wait to get there.

More than 50 earthquakes of varying degrees of severity are reported every day. (Psalm 114:7) The mountains will shake (*Volcanoes*), and the seas will be troubled! (*Tsunamis*, Psalm 46:3) The number of volcanoes erupting now is greater than the 20th century's yearly average. The increase of tsunamis over the last half-century has resulted in more deaths and destruction than ever before.

The hills will melt like wax! (*Extreme heat*, Psalm 97:5) Monster wildfires rage all across the United States. This year in India, 2500 perished because of extreme heat. Another 1229 died in Pakistan. Temperatures in Madrid, Spain, soared to 44 Celsius. The rest of Europe was not any better. Fears rise and people are afraid that next year will be even worse as drought begins to take hold. Climate change, increased temperatures, is the talk of the world as countries scramble to stop what the Lord said was unstoppable.

There are coming more signs in the sun, moon and stars! (Luke 21:25) The sun will go dark and the moon will no longer give light! (Mark 13:25) That means freezing cold temperatures! Meteor showers to be followed by asteroids descending as the powers of heaven are shaken! (Luke 21:26) Then, the very stars themselves will be seen falling from their courses. (Matthew 24:29) Wormwood (*bitterness*), the star of Revelation 8:11, is already on a collision course with man!

Rome is fully aware of this and has been observing the heavens searching for it. Wikipedia reports: "The Vatican Observatory (*Specola Vaticana*) is an astronomical research and educational institution supported by the Holy See. Originally based in the Roman College of Rome, the Observatory is now headquartered in Castel Gandolfo, Italy and operates a telescope at the Mount Graham International Observatory in the United States."

Other signs of the end include an increase of knowledge around the world. (Daniel 12:4) Through the internet or Cloud Computing, knowledge has increased exponentially in the past few years.

Hosea 4:3 tells us that, "the land will mourn, the beasts of the field, and the fowls of heaven and the fish of the sea will be taken away." During the last few years, we have seen fish, birds and other animals die in huge numbers. Since 2010, millions of fish have turned up dead in lakes, rivers and the sea. Birds are seen dropping out of the sky.

When will all these things take place? We have read that they are already beginning all around us? This will culminate in the end of an unbelieving world. When these things come to pass, the day of grace will be coming to an end. Judgment will come upon all who have turned their backs on the wonderful gift of free grace offered. Their end will be in a Christ-less eternity where there will be weeping and wailing and gnashing of teeth. (Matthew 23:13)

For the believer, the story does not end there. With the conclusion of the eighth vision with the justice of God satisfied then comes the crowning.

"Then take silver and gold, and make crowns, and set them upon the head of Joshua the son of Josedech, the high priest;

And speak unto him, saying, Thus speaketh the LORD of hosts, saying, Behold the man whose name is The BRANCH; and he shall grow up out of his place, and he shall build the temple of the LORD." (Zachariah 6:11-12)

This is representative of the coronation of the righteous BRANCH, Jesus, at the end of time! Joshua, the type of Christ, was crowned! Jesus will be crowned! (Jeremiah 23:5) Even his name is typical of Christ. Joshua in Hebrew is Yeshua; in English it is Jesus! When the Master comes, He will not be wearing a crown of thorns, He will be wearing a crown fitting His office. King of Kings and Lord of lords! He will build the final temple! He will rule and reign in a Kingdom that will know no end. (Luke 1:33) Today, the message of the coming Kingdom needs preaching as never before. These are the days of our final preparation and the hour we need to heed the "Final Warning."

When will He come again? No man knows, only The Father. (Mark 13:32) In spite of this fact, many claim they know when He will come! False prophets the world over blatantly announce dates. Others say that the Lord is delaying His coming. Where is His promised

162

appearance? These are scoffers walking after their own lusts. (2 Peter 3:4)

However, we do need to know that His coming is very close. That too has been corrupted by false teachers. They have taught the eventual return of the Lord, to the neglect of the imminent return, as taught by Scripture. Know of a certainty that it might happen even before you turn the last page of this book. Are you ready?

Some teach that there is coming a last great awakening. An awakening, they say, that will sweep the nations like a wildfire. The Bible tells us:

"Let no man deceive you by any means: for that day shall not come, except there come a falling away first, and that man of sin be revealed, the son of perdition." (2 Timothy 2:3)

We have had seven great historic revivals in the past. Seven is the number of completion. The next great revival, the eighth and final awakening, may come during the Tribulation. The church of our generation will then be gone. During that time, the Holy Ghost will continue to touch the hearts of the people of Israel and many will come home. They will look on Him as Yeshua Ha Mashiach, Jesus the Messiah!

"And I will pour upon the house of David, and upon the inhabitants of Jerusalem, the spirit of grace and of supplications: and they shall look upon me whom they have pierced, and they shall mourn for him, as one mourneth for his only son, and shall be in bitterness for him, as one that is in bitterness for his firstborn." (Zachariah 12:10)

Did you notice those words? "They shall look upon me whom they have pierced." That is Jesus Himself speaking to unbelievers, the world over, from the Old

163

Testament. This will be the Tribulation revival of Revelation 7:4.

Many in error claim that in the tribulation the Holy Spirit will be gone. Nothing could be further from the truth. Their confusion comes about from a misinterpretation of 2 Thessalonians 2:7.

"For the mystery of lawlessness is already at work. Only he who now restrains it will do so until he is out of the way."

What this means is that the Holy Spirit holds back "the lawless one," the Antichrist, as long as the Lord wills it. Further, it's the Holy Ghost who convicts the world of sin. (John 16:8) If the Spirit is taken out at the rapture, how then will those who come to Jesus during the tribulation be convicted of sin? How will the 144,000 get saved? (Revelation 7:4) Some say He will do that from heaven but if that was the case, then why is this not the way it happens today? He would not have to be here. The truth is that the Holy Spirit was given to the church to empower her now and those in the tribulation. (Zachariah 4:6) Empowerment will certainly be needed then to stand in the midst of all that is coming!

We have learned that Zachariah received eight visions, teeming with love. Visions that have outlined for us who Jesus is and how He will bring about the end. Eight is a wonderful number and worth taking a look at before we bring this "Final Warning" to a close.

The meaning of the number "Eight" "The eighth king" according to demonic eschatology is the rise of the Antichrist. The meaning described by love in the Bible is "New Beginnings." The eighth day was the first day after God rested. There are seven days in a week and the eighth day is a new beginning. Jesus rose on the Sunday, the first day of the week. Seven days of the previous week and resurrection day was number eight which was a new beginning of the world. (Mark 16:9) When the whole earth was covered with the flood, it was Noah, the eighth person, (2 Peter 2:5) who stepped out onto a new earth to commence a new order of things. Eight souls (1 Peter 3:20) passed through to the new or re-generated world. Circumcision is to be performed on the eighth day (Genesis 17:12) because it was the foreshadowing of the true circumcision of the heart to come. (Colossians 2:11) This is all connected with the new creation. The first-born was given to God on the eighth day. (Exodus 22: 29-30) The Feast of Tabernacles lasts seven days, (*the number of completion*) then comes "Shemini Atzeret" on the eighth day after the sudden end of the feast. (Leveticus.23:36, Numbers 29:35)

Earlier, we learned that there have been seven great historic revivals in the history of the church. Preachers and church leaders all around the world believe we are about to step into the eighth and final awakening, "The Tribulation Revival." During the revivals of history, there were signs in the sun, moon and stars as the presence of the Lord filled the churches. Many of those happened during the periods of what are called tetrads or series of four blood moons.

Four full blood moons do not happen very often, especially connected with the Feasts of the Lord. When they have taken place, awesome things have happened in Israel. Just one example is the rebirth of Israel when a tetrad occurred in conjunction with Passover in 1948. Over the years, seven such tetrads have occurred. Seven back-to-back, blood-red moons fell on the first day of Passover and Sukkoth. (*Tabernacles*)

Are the signs in the sun, moon and stars happening above us today, signaling that something very special is about to happen? On September 28th, 2015 there was another tetrad in conjunction with the Feast of Tabernacles. Did this signal that the end will soon come? Watch out for Russia moving within Syria! Soon their bombing runs will solidify their relations with Iran even more.

Is there coming an unexpected tetrad, four full blood moons that will be accompanied by the last trumpet call? (1 Corinthians 15:52) Remember Jesus said that He would come unexpectedly as a thief in the night. (2 Peter 3:10) Will there be time to finish reading this book? What other signs are there today that the end is upon us?

"This know also, that in the last days perilous times shall come.

For men shall be lovers of their own selves, covetous, boasters, proud, blasphemers, disobedient to parents, unthankful, unholy,

Without natural affection, trucebreakers, false accusers, incontinent, fierce, despisers of those that are good,

Traitors, heady, highminded, lovers of pleasures more than lovers of God;

Having a form of godliness, but denying the power thereof: from such turn away." (2 Timothy 3:1-5)

Are we living in perilous times? Let's look at a few examples of what is happening today. There are uprisings all around the world, with people protesting and rioting and governments toppling. Christians are beheaded, burned alive, or shot and tossed into ditches. The people are starting to see the power they have if they

166

get together. Its Nimrod's referred to oneness in the end times!

Mass killings go unchecked. Historic flooding in the United States again is making headlines. Looting happens daily wherever a crisis strikes at the heart of communities. These are very dangerous times and one that may lead law enforcement to bring in the beast's mark. (Revelation 13:16)

Where can we find lovers of pleasure? Do we live in a world full of pleasure seekers? All we have to do is take a look to the church! A great majority of professing Christians love pleasure more than they love God. They fill their lives with television, partying, socializing, playing games, wasting time on social networks like Facebook, Twitter, Pinterest or Instagram, and God gets only a little of their time. Those going down in the darkness for the last time are non-starters, when it comes to getting the attention of some church people.

We certainly live in a covetous age, where people clamor after the biggest and best of everything. The majority of people today seek after worldly riches, rather than eternal, heavenly riches. (Matthew 6:19-20) Many claim that possessions are a great testimony of the goodness of God in their lives. Yet, they turn their backs on the hungry and destitute in our cities. They care little for that tiny child who goes to bed hungry at night! It's heartbreaking when people say, "send them to the food bank or give them the address of the Welfare Office, that's what they are there for." Whatever happened to the poor being fed by the church and not the state in compliance with the biblical norm?

Where do the proud find their hiding place? Pride was the original sin that caused Satan to fall from his exalted position in heaven, and pride is the sin that most people cherish in this world today. They are found in their places at church. When giving testimony, 98 percent is about how bad they were and only two percent about the goodness of God. Others spend a fortune promoting their ministries; "see me," they shout from the mountain tops!

Are our children disobedient to their parents? The youth of today goes about in gangs, having little respect for their elders or parents, and pretty much little respect for anything. Why is that? It's because society today teaches them that going to church is alright, but they can continue doing their own thing with their friends. "Cheap-grace!" They have no idea what Jesus Christ has done for them. Where are the witnesses, where are the preachers of real grace? Most people are at some meeting seeking a manifestation or at home soaking, and not searching for and rescuing the perishing.

Can we find un-thankfulness anywhere today? The world and the church have so conditioned us to take things for granted. Are we really thankful to God for the many blessings He has bestowed upon us? Or do we just take things for granted and demand more? If Christians are unthankful, then what are those outside the faith like? Spare a thought for our Jesus, who paid sin's price to buy us back!

It's so sad to say that holiness is absent in many churches. Go back just 50 years and we would find a world with Christians who were far more humble and holy. Many in our day believe and teach that we don't need to keep the Ten Commandments anymore, just as long as we believe in Jesus. The "hyper-grace" message says: Once we have been forgiven it doesn't matter how

168

we live, we have grace! What does this lead to? People continuing to live in sin and live unholy lives. Jude 1:4 tells us:

"For there are certain men crept in unawares, who were before of old ordained to this condemnation, ungodly men, turning the grace of our God into lasciviousness, and denying the only Lord God, and our Lord Jesus Christ."

As a result, churches today have become more like social clubs, theatres and concert halls, rather than holy places of worship!

Even our governments have made it lawful for people to live without natural affection. Earlier we read how homosexuality and lesbianism is pushed and accepted all around the world. In fact, it has become the established norm in many places. Even government leaders scream support for same-sex marriage, just like Prime Minister Stephen Harper by his silence on the issue. He also said that the issue of same-sex marriage will not be revisited by his political party, despite the fact that some in his own party oppose it.

We also have churches who not only advocate it, they ordain practicing homosexuals and lesbians!

Where are those who despise those that are good? We live in an age today where people will not take loving correction or rebuke for their sins. They cannot tolerate those who speak up for truth in love and the whole counsel of God's Word. If someone warns Christians of their error, they themselves become outcasts. They are branded as being of the devil. They are ostracized and kept from being effective. The battle of the hour is a war that rages against the truth of God's ultimate revelation, which is the fulfillment of all things in Jesus, the way to salvation.

Alas, there is a price to pay for the truth and I for one, am willing to pay that price.

It's a price paid by Kim Davis of Rowan County, Kentucky, U.S.A. Authorities detained her for contempt of a Supreme Court ruling for refusing to issue same-sex marriage licenses. Of course Satan's accepting groups said she deserved jail as government officials have no right to have their faith dictate government policy. They could have simply fired her and got another to do the job. They did not! Obviously the actions of the court and legal system in her community are being dictated to by hell. This hero of the faith was willing to pay the price for standing up for truth. As she gallantly stood fast, people who despise those that are good attacked her. Their plans failed!

Lovers of themselves, where are they? These signs of the last days so clearly speak about our generation. Do people love themselves today by putting themselves before God and other people? Most certainly! We seem more concerned about how we look on the outside, rather than how we look on the inside. It's for this reason that people in churches want the external rather than the internal where Jesus begins His work and they could care less that they stand in the presence of the Eternal.

Everything is commercialized to the extreme to make people think about ME, ME, ME! When worship teams are more interested in click tracks, head or foot signals, audio quality, instead of drawing people into the presence of the Lord, they are lovers of themselves. When they spend more time in the music stores picking out the next best thing rather than in prayer. What would we call it?

Having a form of Godliness, but denying the power is everywhere around us. Glitter clouds, orbs of light, so-called angel feathers, oil on the hands, Theophostic Therapy, Theophostic Prayer Ministry, Sozo Ministry, spirit writing and Prophetic Prayer Ministry are nothing compared to the Glory Cloud filling the house that Moses could not even enter. (Exodus 40:35) Let me remind you again of the day when Moses came down from the mountain, he had to put a bag over his head because the glory was too much for the people! (Exodus 34:33) How do any of the so-called manifestations today compare to the heart of the Word of God? In this many have a form of Godliness, but deny the full power of God that is available to us!

Nothing can match the sound of newborn babies crying at our altars, yet these are few and far between. Why, because we can only reproduce after our own kind. (Genesis 1:11) Perhaps the Lord is saying He does not want churches today reproducing after their kind. In the Old Testament, it was a shame being barren. Today the empty church seats are proof positive we are barren. The shame of it though, does not seem to touch the heart of church leadership beyond the fact of reduced offerings. Evangelism has been relegated to a bottom line in the church budget.

Today, revival is a word bandied about by many. Every time it's used, it seems to carry us further and further away from true historic revival. Many of them only have that "form" of Godliness and are not filled with the true Spirit of God. Anyone can rent a stadium! Put an elaborate "Christian" rock band on stage! Say "nice"

171

things to make people feel good! Draw many people through the doors and call it "revival!" Do we really know what true revival is?

It's when there is a turning away from sin and a return to living holy lives for God. It's when people flock to the altar in their masses, broken over the sin in their lives. It's them walking away, saved, healed and delivered with every ounce of worldly hurt surrendered to the Lord! The so-called revivals happening today are nothing more than worldly excitement.

If these truths, these promised signs of the end times, do not convince us that the end has come, consider these last few realities. If this has not been enough to encourage us to heed "the Final Warning." Consider that at the time of the end, there is coming a massive army!

"And the number of the armies of the horsemen was two hundred million; I heard the number of them." (Revelation 9:16)

An army of that size never existed until China's army reached that number in the 1960s. Right now they stand poised along with North Korea to come pouring out of their borders. They are ready to link up with Iran and the other nations of the Gog, Magog Alliance.

Presently, one of the last pieces of the puzzle is coming together! Ezekiel, chapters 40-48, speaks of both the Tribulation Temple and the Millennial Temple. One of the greatest debates today is where the Tribulation Temple will be built. Many argue that it has to be built on "the Dome of the Rock." Others say this can't be because it's a Muslim shrine and according to Jewish law cannot be destroyed. This flies in the face of the political voices being raised in Israel, calling for its immediate destruction. Others say it can only be built when Messiah comes! All are in for a great shock!

The proper identity of the "Rock" which many believe is the Dome of the Rock will truly be a revelation to all modern religious groups when they discover the truth of its biblical relevance. Amazement will take hold of the church when they realize that "the Dome of the Rock" was not the site of the former Temples of Solomon, Zerubbabel and Herod. The builders erected them on a different rock, a "Rock" purely of Christian importance and it was formerly recognized by Christians until the seventh century and even historically until the time of the Crusades. The original site was a most prominent Christian site which John singled out in his Gospel as a "Rock, pavement, stone, Strong's G3038," (John 19:13) that dealt directly with Christ Jesus and His mission to this earth. The early Christians, Jews and Muslims knew this. The Dome of the Rock built by Abd Al-Malik in 692 A.D. was designed to direct Christians away from that "Rock" and orient them toward the newly constructed Al Aqsa Mosque (*which they reckoned was the re-christened Muslim Temple of Solomon*) located near the south wall of the Haram esh-Sharif. In this, they intended to further lead Christians directly to the city of Mecca, where Allah (*the Arabic for "their god"*) then had symbolic residence. The Dome of the Spirits, the real site, was actually a little more to the north of the Dome of the Rock.

The noted Archaeologist, Asher Kaufman, a Physicist, agrees entirely with this conclusion. Dr. Kaufman, formerly of the Racah Institute of Physics, Hebrew University, Jerusalem, for many years made careful studies on Mount Moriah leading him to believe,

173

"the Temples of Solomon and Zerubbabel were both located just north of the Dome of the Rock on the paved platform area. The Holy of Holies many believe was on the bedrock covered by a small shrine, the Dome of the Spirits. The Muslim stewards of the site have systematically destroyed or covered over all evidence that the site was once important to the Jews or to Christians."

All of this may have been an attempt by evil men who understood prophecy to delay the future building of the Temple. (Daniel 10:13) Their efforts were defeated right from the outset as all of us will see by soon to be fulfilled prophecy. The temple can now be built!

One of the things required by Scripture for the restored temple is a red heifer. This is mandatory for the rebirth of sacrificial purification. The book of Numbers records:

"This is the ordinance of the law which the LORD hath commanded, saying, Speak unto the children of Israel, that they bring thee a red heifer without spot, wherein, is no blemish, and upon which never came yoke:

And ye shall give her unto Eleazar the priest that he may bring her forth without the camp, and one shall slay her before his face:

And Eleazar the priest shall take of her blood with his finger, and sprinkle of her blood directly before the tabernacle of the congregation seven times:

And one shall burn the heifer in his sight; her skin, and her flesh, and her blood, with her dung, shall he burn:

And the priest shall take cedar wood, and hyssop, and scarlet, and cast it into the midst of the burning of the heifer.

Then the priest shall wash his clothes, and he shall bathe his flesh in water, and afterward he shall come into the camp, and the priest shall be unclean until the even." (Numbers 19: 2-7)

The red heifer, a type of Christ, will be required at the temple building, to be used in the process of purification described in the book of Numbers. In May 1997 the first pure red Heifer was born in 2000 years. Another red Heifer was born in Israel in March of 2002.

"The Temple Institute in Jerusalem has announced that it has finished building an altar suitable for the Temple service. The altar, which took several years to build, can be operational at little more than a moment's notice," reported Matzav Haruach Magazine.

The stage has been set! The players are gathering all around the globe! What will we do with the words of this "Final Warning?" We can discard them into the garbage! We can rip them apart looking for some loophole to continue in our belief, or we can search the Word to see if these things are so! (Acts 17:11) The choice is ours! No one can make up our minds for us!

Right now my heart is breaking. I have only a few words left to reach your heart. To have you run to Jesus before it's too late! This book has been one of truth as God has given me the light to see His truth. So, I end this book as it began with a Word of Life.

"When I say unto the wicked, Thou shalt surely die; and thou givest him not warning, nor speakest to warn the wicked from his wicked way, to save his life; the same wicked man shall die in his iniquity; but his blood will I require at thine hand.

Yet if thou warn the wicked, and he turn not from his wickedness, nor from his wicked way, he shall die in his iniquity; but thou hast delivered thy soul." (Ezekiel 3: 18-19)

In love I have brought you, "the Final Warning." I ask you to let these last words sink deep inside your heart.

"I call heaven and earth to record this day against you that I have set before you, life and death, blessing and cursing: therefore choose life that both thou and thy seed may live." (Deuteronomy 30:19)

The End

CHOOSING LIFE

Dear reader;

Jesus right now is singing a song of love over you. He is beckoning to you, calling you to the safety of His wings. Time is short. This book has convinced you of that truth.

Suddenly in the twinkling of an eye, we are going be gone to the greatest wedding feast known to humanity. Will you be there or will you be left behind?

To show you how precious you are to Him. To show you how loved you are to Him. He came and gave His life to buy us back from the pit of sin. YOU, yes, you.... Really you! The gift He offers is exactly that, a gift. We don't have to work for it. It's ours just for the asking. He gives it to us by grace through faith in Him. All we have to do is ask Him to come into our heart and life. We come to Him willing to surrender all our plans, hopes and dreams to His care and keeping. Jesus said repent for the Kingdom of heaven is at hand. Repentance that is the only way in through the door to safety. (Matthew 4:17)

If you are one who has been trapped in some sort of error in your church. If you have been confused by the things you have been taught. I want you to know that He was there with you through it all. Just like His precious Israel, you too are the apple of His eye. He is calling you to come out from among them. (2 Corinthians 6:17) All you have to do is come back home to Him. You know the way!

If the Lord has spoken to you through the words of this His, "Final Warning," know that it was written especially for you. If you want to escape all that is coming on the earth, run to Him right now. Pray this simple prayer with me.

'Father, in Jesus name I come to you. I ask you to forgive me for all of my sin. Wash me in the blood of Jesus. Lord Jesus I completely surrender to you my life, my plans, my goals, my future and accept your plans and purposes, for my life. Lord Jesus come into my heart and life and be my Savior and Lord. In Jesus Name.'

If you prayed that prayer and meant business with God, I want you to know that your sins are forgiven and your name is written in the book of life.

If you prayed that prayer I would like to hear from you and pray for you. Jesus is still in the miracle working business and I give you His word. No matter what the need Jesus will meet you at the point of that need.

Please contact me at the phone number, email address or the website below. I would love to hear what Jesus has done in your life.

As a reminder of your decision this day, your very special day then fill in the portion below.

On this date: _____

I (Enter your Name) _____

Accepted Jesus as my Lord and Savior.

Signature: _____

Any time you question your decision open this book, see again your signature and be assured you belong to the Master.

If you have read this book and an anger has risen in your soul. If you cast my name out from your company. If you take this work and toss it in the garbage, know this. You are forgiven! Jesus loves you with an everlasting love and with loving kindness He is drawing you.

I bless you and make a commitment to pray for you as long as life remains within my body. You are very special to the Lord and I love you so very much.

ABOUT THE AUTHOR

George Jenkins is an ordinary guy who has spent a lifetime seeking out deeper truths of the Word of God! He lives in Kitchener, Ontario, Canada, from where he reaches out to fulfill his purpose in life.

George established Kingdom Ministries Canada that reaches locally and around the world. His burden is for the body of Christ, to come together, embracing the task assigned to the church. "That we should earnestly contend for the faith which was once delivered to the saints." (Jude 3, *paraphrased*) George counts serving the ministries of all denominations at home and abroad as one of his greatest privileges in life.

You can reach George at:
7-16 Bonfield Place,
Kitchener, Ontario. Canada. N2E 1H5
Telephone: 519-804-2973
Email: ciskitchener@gmail.com

My sincere thanks to Robert Quehl
The Word Doctor – Kitchener
Editor
Email: worddoctor911@gmail.com

www.ingramcontent.com/pod-product-compliance
Lightning Source LLC
Chambersburg PA
CBHW060242050426
42448CB00009B/1560

What people are saying...

"Imagine the culinary convenience of fine French cuisine available at a drive-through window. Such is the ease with which you will read this succinctly written compilation of petite engaging topics and stories that will provide pleasure and provoke your mind and imagination. Expect to be amused, surprised, motivated, alarmed, and inspired, to chuckle, to groan, to think and to act."

Dr. Ron Unruh, Author and Artist

Body Parts and the Invisible You is an incredible read. Each chapter brings a whole new interest and is a feast of wisdom and insight. The book will inspire, challenge, motivate and encourage you. I highly recommend it."

Peter Lowe, Founder, Get Motivated Seminars and Businesspeople of Faith

"This book is like wine tasting, it is best sampled and savored. Observations are made about our lives, the world and our society, the topics of which lend themselves for discussion with family, friends and professional colleagues. You may find some subjects that you have been avoiding hit too close to home. However, there is much "food for thought" and you may not agree with everything but it is all worth considering. This book is certainly worth the read, but sample a few chapters at a time and savor each one."

Robert Humphries, Ph.D.

"John Murray is a friend I met when he worked with an organization that gave him access to some of the world's most needy and most hurting people. I'm impressed with John's insight into the human soul and his prescription for hope. You'll enjoy his book!"

Dr. Garth Leno, Senior Pastor, The Gathering, Windsor, Ontario

"In this collection of pieces about life's common and not so common experiences, John Murray invites reflection on how we face each day.

Whether he is thinking about a terminally ill friend, acknowledging the challenges caregivers face, or discussing the frequency with which we should eat pumpkin pie, his wide-ranging observations will stimulate your intellectual, emotional and spiritual growth, encouraging you to purposeful living. John excels in finding significant life lessons hiding under the clutter of daily routine."

David Daniels, M.T.S., M.Min. Freelance Writer and Book Reviewer

"John carefully and poignantly covers many practical aspects of life in this book. His wisdom and his own life experiences allow him to challenge the reader to reflect on their own life in a way that does not simply react but encourages the reader to respond to these challenges by proactively pursuing improved and better choices in life. It is truly a very "thought provoking" book that the reader cannot help but reflect on his or her individual journey of life. I highly recommend this book as a must read."

Bill King, President, The Nova Group Inc.

*"**Body Parts and the Invisible You** is full of good advice and wisdom. It points you in the direction of a healthy and whole life, both in body and spirit. It stresses the importance of "living in the now" and being fulfilled in the present. I found the chapter on "caregiving" particularly meaningful. Read the book and be inspired. It has given me the inspiration to write my own book – maybe it will do the same for you!"*

David Carson, B.Sc., PGCE, Director, Intercessors for Canada

"In this compilation of thought-provoking chapters, John has written on a variety of subjects, some of which we would not normally have the time or inclination to pursue. In fact, some topics would bring out an innate reluctance in us to explore. However, if we take up the challenge of thinking through these issues as they relate to the meaning of life, I am convinced they tacitly point to the existence of God, just as a serious consideration of the Divine explains the mystery of life. Enjoy the read!"

David North, B.Ed., M.Ed. Retired Principal,
Lions Gate Christian Academy